Religion in America

ADVISORY EDITOR

Edwin S. Gaustad

HISTORICAL SKETCHES
OF THE MISSIONS
OF
THE AMERICAN BOARD

S[amuel] C. Bartlett

ARNO PRESS
A NEW YORK TIMES COMPANY
New York • 1972

50508

Reprint Edition 1972 by Arno Press Inc.

Reprinted from copies in
The State Historical Society of Wisconsin Library

RELIGION IN AMERICA - Series II
ISBN for complete set: 0-405-04050-4
See last pages of this volume for titles.

Manufactured in the United States of America

Library of Congress Cataloging in Publication Data

Bartlett, Samuel Colcord, 1817-1898.
    Historical sketches of the missions of the American
Board.

    (Religion in America, series II)
    Reprint of 6 sketches first published separately
in 1876.
    CONTENTS: In Africa.--In China.--In India and
Ceylon. [etc.]
    1. Missions. I. American Board of Commissioners
for Foreign Missions. II. Title.
BV2750.B37   266'.023 ·   78-38436
ISBN 0-405-04057-1

Contents

Bartlett, S[amuel] C.

HISTORICAL SKETCH

OF THE

MISSIONS OF THE AMERICAN BOARD

IN

AFRICA.

BY

REV. S. C. BARTLETT, D. D.

BOSTON:

PUBLISHED BY THE BOARD,

1 SOMERSET STREET.

1876.

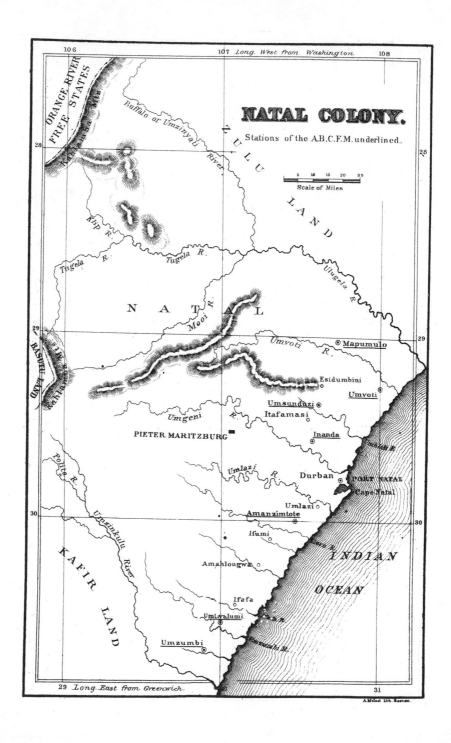

NATAL COLONY.

Stations of the A.B.C.F.M. underlined.

Scale of Miles

ORANGE RIVER FREE STATES

ZULU LAND

Buffalo or Umzinyati River.

Klip R.

Tugela R.

Tugela R.

Ulugela R.

NATAL

Mooi R.

Umvoti R.

Mapumulo

Esidumbini

Umvoti

BASUTU LAND

Umgeni R.

Umsunduzi

Itafamasi

PIETER MARITZBURG

Inanda

Polla R.

Umlazi R.

Durban

PORT NATAL

Cape Natal.

Umzinkulu River

Umlazi

Amanzimtote

KAFIR LAND

Ifumi

INDIAN

OCEAN

Amahlongwa

Ifafa

Umtwalumi

Umzumbi

Umzumbi R.

106   107 Long. West from. Washington   108

28   28

29   29

30   30

29 Long. East from Greenwich.   31

A.McLeod Lith. Boston.

BARTLETT'S SKETCHES

MISSIONS IN AFRICA.

AFRICA has been a dark land. Excepting the extreme northern part, its history is unknown. Its surface was long wholly unexplored. Its moral condition was gloomy, and its prospects forbidding. Its coast line, without bays or peninsulas, was repellent. Malignant fevers stood sentinel along its rivers. Petty fighting tribes were a terror to the traveler, and a hundred and fifty dialects a bar to the missionary. Among its explorers, Horne-mann, Oudney, Clapperton, Overweg, Duncan, Ritchie, and probably Livingston, have perished, and Park, Neu-wied, Laing, Vogel, and Maguire have been murdered.

And yet nature has dealt lavishly with Africa. It is indeed the land of great deserts and of torrid heat. The sands of Guinea and of Nubia will roast an egg or blister a negro's foot; but the vegetable and animal life of the continent are marvelous in abundance, variety, and magnificence. Its species of quadrupeds are three times as many as those of America, and five times those of Asia. The most brilliant birds, the most beautiful insects, the hugest reptiles, and the lordliest brutes abound. Fruits, grain, spices, and vegetable products in immense variety, fill its interior. In Yoruba, says a traveler, "the hill-sides and banks of streams often present the appearance of solid walls of leaves and flowers. The grass on the

1

prairies is from eight to twelve feet high, and almost impervious." And at Natal you " can find flowers every month in the year, and at times so thick in the open fields that scarce a step could be taken without treading some of them under foot."

Lowest and meanest of its productions are its human beings. With exceptions, the races of Africa seem best fitted to show how nearly a man may sink to an animal. Nothing is too low to worship. Slavery is the most ancient inheritance of the country. The chief coast trade for ages was in slaves ; and systems of brigandage were organized all through the interior to supply the market. Polygamy of the lowest, loosest kind is universal. For an ox or two the husband buys his wife, and for a string of beads the mother has sold her child into bondage. The frightful prevalence of cannibalism was checked by the greater value of the victim for the slave market than the table. Everywhere woman is the animal of all work, and in many tribes modesty in personal exposure is almost unknown. The traveler beholds " young women dabbling in the creeks," innocent of clothing and of scruples.

Yet all that was forbidding in Africa has not repelled the missionary, nor prevented his success. More than twenty different Boards have planted stations in this moral waste. They have found the people highly susceptible to religious influences, wherever rum, war, and the slave trade would permit those influences to act. They reckon some forty-seven thousand communicants at the present time, many of them, however, in churches that do not make conversion a condition of church membership. Many a thrilling story could be told of the labors and adventures of such men as Vanderkemp, Shaw, the Albrechts, Krapf, and Moffatt. It was hard at times for Moffatt to know whether he was safer among the Bechuanas by day, or among the eight lions that roared around his wagon in one night. It would be delightful to sketch some of the remarkable revivals that have visited the Methodist, Wesleyan, Moravian, Baptist, and Presbyterian missions, and to portray some of the Christian lives they have wrought, and the transformations of society. But we leave the tempting field for the humbler work of the American Board.

The missions of the Board have been two — the Gaboon mission in West Africa, near the equator, and the Zulu mission in South Africa, toward the Cape. They are interesting in quality rather than in quantity. They show how the gospel can struggle with the mightiest of obstacles, and what it can do for the most degraded of characters.

The Gaboon mission need not detain us long. Its operations have been small, obstructed, and interrupted ; and the mission is now transferred to the Presbyterian Board. In the year 1834, John Leighton Wilson landed at Cape Palmas to explore the place where, in the following year, he landed with his wife, and was received with joyful acclamations by the natives. Here he erected a framed house, which he had brought from America, opened a school, and began a book in the native tongue. Other missionaries followed — Messrs. White, Walker, Griswold, and Alexander Wilson, with their wives. The mission was headed for the interior. The plan was to make this the entering-wedge for a great system of inland operations.

It is scarcely possible for a Christian American to conceive the degradation of these Guinea negroes. Their

P

morals were blacker than their skins. Mr. Wilson has drawn a large portrait of them with such strokes as these : " Falsehood is universal. Chastity is an idea for which they have no word, and of which they can scarcely form a conception." And after enumerating almost every varied form of vice, he concludes, " It is almost impossible to say what vice is pre-eminent." But even with such a people the gospel proved " the power of God." Twenty-three of them were in due time converted and added to the church. A large boarding-school was filled with pupils, and day schools established at seven stations. Mr. Wilson at one time had a native audience of six hundred persons ; but the embarrassments of the Board in 1837 first crippled the mission ; and collisions with the neighboring American colony from Maryland, which Mr. Wilson had once saved from the fury of the natives, after seven years compelled a removal to the Gaboon. Here Satan's kingdom had not then been introduced from other lands — only the *fetishes* and native devils of Africa were the foes. There was no foreign government within five hundred miles on either side, and no trading factory along the shore. Nobler races, the Mpongwes and Bakeles, gave the missionaries a warm welcome. Scarcely was the work under way when, in two years, three French ships of war entered the river, and by brandy and fraud bought the territory. French guns even endangered the lives of the missionaries, and French influence reigned over the region. Still converts came dropping in — six, nine, twelve, eighteen in a year. Christian assemblies were organized. Two dialects were reduced to writing. More than a hundred youths gained a Christian education, and many thousands received light enough for salvation. Precious missionary martyrs — Mr. and Mrs.

White, Mr. and Mrs. Griswold, Mr. and Mrs. Porter, Dr. Wilson, Mrs. Walker, Mrs. Bushnell — cheerfully laid down their lives. But while the relations of the French authorities ultimately became pleasant, they were the cover for introducing Romish missionaries and all the unutterable abominations of the foreign trade. English, Scotch, and Dutch trading factories, and native dram-shops, crowded the shore, and a medley of tribes from every quarter rushed thither. The foreign captain, who had left a white wife perhaps in New England, hired an ebony wife or wives " by the week," or " by the run," in Africa. Rum became the presiding demon of the region. "Satan," said a missionary, " has an agent in every foreigner in the river." Well might he say it, when even " a Scotch Presbyterian elder sent a hundred thousand gallons of ' liquid damnation ' to the heathen in a single vessel, and atoned for the whole by giving a missionary free passage." " It is these things that kill," wrote the missionary. Yea, they killed! Year after year these and kindred influences corrupted the whole community and the native church members. In 1868, seventeen were excommunicated at one time, nearly all of whom commenced their downward course in connection with rum. " The missionary works at the entrance of Ge-henna," writes Mr. Walker in 1869 ; and his wail is echoed by the deliberate utterance of a Scotch missionary on the western coast, " *But for the British rum trade*, I feel confident that long ere this the native membership of the church at Duke Town would have been reckoned by hundreds instead of tens."

Never was a more formidable struggle. It was one long conflict, not alone or chiefly with African heathen-ism, but with the outlawed vices of the French, English,

American, Dutch, and Scotch nations. But in this Africo-European "Gehenna," the devoted missionaries never gave up heart or hope. After a quarter of a century of buffeting with Satan in his citadel, Mr. Walker could say, "I desire to live to see the Gaboon mission in a different condition. I have faith in God. I believe that he will perform all his grand promises. The gospel is still the power of God unto salvation." The latest report of the mission announces the boys' school and the girls' school still in encouraging operation, six accessions to the church, and Sabbath congregations "as attentive as any in the States." Still the church is but a shadow of what it should have been. Mr. Walker has retired after his twenty-eight years of toil and conflict, and the mission is transferred to the Presbyterian Board, with a prayer for God's blessing on it.

The Zulu mission is a brighter field, though the fiery ordeal has swept over it. It deals with a higher style of man. The Zulus, an offshoot of the Caffre stock, stand midway between the negro and the European type. The black skin and woolly hair are joined often with the aquiline nose, straight lip, prominent forehead, mild eye and lithe and muscular physique. The scantiness of their costume — ranging from nothing up to a greased cow-skin demi-skirt — is compensated for by a profusion of bracelets, armlets, anklets, necklaces, girdles, shoulder-bands, and rings for the ears, fingers, and thumbs. The people live in *kraals*, or circles of wicker-work beehive houses, thatched with grass, and floored with mixed ants' nests and cow-dung. The men take care of the cattle, do the tailoring for themselves and wives, lounge, drink, smoke, snuff, and when food is plenty, gorge like boa-constrictors; while the poor woman, " with her pickaxe and basket, must serve as plow and cart, horse and ox," corn planter, grist-mill, and cook. In other words, woman was virtually a slave. They were brimful of superstitions, with witchcrafts and witch doctors, the latter wielding practically the power of life and death; and they worshiped the spirits of their ancestors. In these huts, infested with cockroaches, and in cold weather filled with soot and smoke, imagine them round the central fire, seated on their haunches, like the dogs by their side, snuffing, smoking, eating, chattering, and laughing till bed-time, then dropping on their rush mat and block pillow, covered with a hide, while goats, sheep, and calves share their hut, — and you partly apprehend the case.

Such was the inviting scene which, in 1834, six missionaries set forth to see. They were Rev. Messrs. A. Grout, Champion, Lindley, Wilson, Venable, and Dr. Adams, with their wives. But they were not at once to be gratified. One company of them designed to stay at Port Natal, the other to strike for the interior. The latter party traveled a thousand miles in ox teams, only to be driven back by the *Boers*, or half-savage Dutch farmers, over wretched roads, thirteen hundred miles in length, — leaving the lifeless form of Mrs. Wilson till the resurrection. Mrs. Grout, of the coast party, had died of consumption soon after landing in Africa.

Meanwhile the coast party had begun their work at Umlazi, near Port Natal. While Messrs. Grout and Adams were conveying their families and goods to the place, Mr. Champion opened a school. His first school-house was the shade of a tree; his first school-book was the sand, in which he traced the letters; and of his first twelve scholars, some were nurses, with infants tied to their backs. Three other stations were occupied a few months later. Two schools, with fifty scholars, were already established, a printing press in operation, and a Sabbath congregation of five hundred persons gathered, when the storm of a war between the Dutch farmers and the Zulus broke upon them, and drove them away. Four years later a part of them returned and resumed the broken work. The printing press was working again in the scorched mission buildings at Umlazi, a flourishing school gathered, a Sabbath school of two hundred, and a congregation of five hundred; and, O, joy! at last there was one hopeful convert. A second station at Empangeni numbered an audience of two or three hundred, in the centre of thirty-seven kraals, when, one morning, at daybreak, a sudden attack from King Dingan, on six of the nearer kraals, doomed three of them to utter destruction. Though no harm was done to the missionary, it was an act of distinct hostility to the mission, and of retaliation for its growing influence over Dingan's subjects. Mr. Grout declined the unequal contest, and left the field. In view of these repeated disasters, and the unsettled state of the country, the Prudential Committee determined to abandon it.

Here seemed the end of nine years' labor. But Providence interposed. Natal meanwhile passed under British control. The natives began to flock thither for protection, till ten thousand of them had collected; and it became clear that the government was about to pursue an honorable policy. When Mr. Grout reached Cape Town, on his way home, he was met by a united remonstrance from Christians and ministers of every denomination, as well as from the American consul and the British governor. A public meeting was called, and a year's support for Mr. Grout was raised. The post of government missionaries was offered to Messrs. Grout and Adams, and of government preacher among the Boers to Mr. Lindley.

The Board recognized the plain interposition, and revoked their instructions. The missionaries turned joyfully to their work. After ten years of toil, a solitary convert at Umlazi — an old woman — sat down with Mr. and Mrs. Adams to the table of the Lord. Six months later, two men came out from heathenism and polygamy, and took each one wife in Christian marriage. At the end of the year still another. The long-deferred harvest was begun.

Re-enforcements came. Six years after the mission was on the point of being abandoned, it comprised thirteen missionaries — Adams, A. Grout, Lindley, Bryant, L. Grout, McKinney, Rood, Marsh, Ireland, Abraham, Tyler, Wilder, Dohne — with their wives, laboring hopefully at twelve stations. Nine churches had been organized, containing one hundred and twenty-three members, thirty-six of whom were received in one year. But trials were not over. The young school of teachers and preachers that was started in 1853 with nine scholars, and in four years increased to twenty-five, was broken up by the failure of Mr. Rood's health. In the great discussion of polygamy in 1855 and 1856, Bishop Colenso defended the system. The disturbed state of the country for several years hindered religious interest. The missionaries toiled on. A Zulu Dictionary of ten thousand words appeared, and a Grammar of four hundred and thirty pages. The Scriptures were printed by gradual installments, beginning with the historic portions of the New Testament. School books of various kinds ap-

peared. Steady congregations were gained and held.
By the end of 1863, such palpable signs as these were
seen : two hundred and sixty-six church members in
good standing; one hundred and seventy-five Christian
families, comprising five hundred baptized children; several congregations of from one hundred to three hundred,
three fourths of them respectably clad, worshiping in
brick buildings erected chiefly by the natives; two native
home missionaries, supported by native converts; schools
maintained by the natives; prayer meetings well sustained, and monthly concerts, with contributions averaging a dollar a year to each member; many families
living in brick houses, with nearly all the appliances of
civilized life; a hundred Yankee plows at work in the
fields, to the inexpressible relief of poor, toiling woman.
These things were palpable to the eye.

The year 1865 brought a cheering revival like those
of the home churches, and, sooner or later, of all the
missions. Its extent was not great; yet it brought seventy-nine converts into the churches in a single year.
The same year witnessed the establishment of a permanent training-school for teachers, and measures for a
boarding-school for girls. And when, next year, Mr.
Grout saw three native preachers supported by the native
missionary society, and a thousand dollars of native contributions; ninety-seven members in his own church, and
an average of four hundred in his congregation — he who
had been driven away from three successive stations, and
waited eleven years for his first convert — well might he
exclaim, "If I was a fool in the eyes of some men, I
have lived to see a hundred fold more done than I ever
dreamed that I might effect in a long life, and have enjoyed a hundred fold more than I expected. Every

promise of God has been abundantly fulfilled to me." It was written in the very year when Bishop Colenso said, " the plan of salvation was so difficult, he never tried to explain it to the Zulus."

The good work has gone steadily, if not rapidly, forward. The annual report for 1870 shows nineteen stations and out-stations, with twelve churches, containing about five hundred members, twenty-eight of whom were received within the year. The little band of missionaries, — apostolic in number, — with their fifteen female assistant missionaries, are at length re-enforced by thirteen native preachers and two native pastors — one of them rejoicing in the honored name of Rufus Anderson, — eighteen teachers and four catechists, eighteen common schools, a female seminary with twenty-six bright-eyed, quick-witted girls ; the training-school, with its thirty-five young men, — its British aid of one thousand dollars a year, and its expanding plans, — give cheering promise that the harvest-time is not far away. Meanwhile, where once were only kraals, the visitor would now see more than two hundred upright houses, a dozen of them built of brick ; children engaged with their books, or perhaps praying in the bush ; readers of the Pilgrim's Progress and the Dairyman's Daughter, translated by a Zulu girl ; students of Barnes's Notes ; congregations that can sing, " Nearer, my God, to Thee ; " school girls that will repeat a psalm or hymn without mistake, after a single hearing — one of whom learned the first seven psalms in half an hour. He would hear a dying mother say, " I know I am dying ; but why should I fear to go home? I love my Saviour. I love my God. I have no fear — all is so bright." He might see a man in the prime of life who has abandoned Zulu wealth and power,· and resisted the dissuasions and almost compulsions of his friends to travel with the gospel message to many hundreds of his fellows, ever hearing those words, "Son of man, I have set thee for a watchman." He could see, in the day schools at Mapumulo, four grandchildren of a man who once refused to send his own children, lest they should become Christians, while one of those very sons now takes part in the prayer meeting. In those African schools you might see a girl with eight spear-marks on her person; another who was untied from the back of her dead mother in the waters; another who fled from the den of the polygamist, to which she had been sold for two extra cows; a young man whose tribe-mark is an amputated finger; and another whose relatives once burned his clothes, and intoxicated him by force, to keep him away. "These are they which came out of great tribulation."

Or you might take a walk with a lady missionary to the homes of the Christian Zulus around her. Passing the white cottage flanked by rows of orange trees, where the wife is away, — though the husband, dressed in his straw hat, blue shirt, and black trousers, invites you in, — you enter the next house, where the mother, in calico dress, sits sewing with the baby by her, and a boy and girl sit by the table, one with a book, the other with the needle, while the room contains chairs, book-shelves, and a cupboard, with cups and saucers, and the bed-room adjoining shows a bed with its blankets, and pillows, and patch-work quilt. The next, a brown cottage, shows a little girl in front teaching the baby to walk. In the parlor a young woman is cutting and making a dress, the father reading aloud, while the wife sits near at work, and some children are playing with a doll. And when you leave, the three-year-old "Jeremiah" will take up the song he heard on Saturday in school. "Beyond, we came to a red-brick house, a flower-garden in front, curtained windows, and matted floor. In the parlor stood a table, with ink, pens, paper, and books on it, and a clock ticked away merrily on the shelf. The table was set for tea in the back room, with cloth, plates, cups and saucers, spoons and forks, bread, butter, and sugar, while hot coffee was ready, of which the cup we drank was very acceptable. I asked the father what he did evenings. 'O,' he said, 'we light the candle, my wife sews, and I teach the children their lessons for school the next day. When this is done, we pray, sing a hymn, I read a chapter, and we go to bed.'"

Reader, these scenes are in Zulu land, these people are jet black, and the kraal is still in sight of their homes. And one of the noble men who began that blessed change, Alden Grout, after thirty-five years of undaunted toil and trial, still lives to thank God for it all; and through eternity will he rejoice in the work God gave him to do.

March, 1876.

The foregoing sketch was prepared in 1871. A new edition being called for, it was thought best to use the stereotype plates as they were, appending here the statistics of the mission as reported for 1875. And it seems needful to do little more than this. The mission has continued its work much as heretofore, except that more attention has been given to touring and the frequent visiting of heathen kraals around the stations. Some of the missionaries have taken special interest in efforts of this kind, in which they have often found much to encourage.

Thoughts have been turned, also, to plans for an extension of the work among other distant and more ignorant
portions of the Zulu race; and Mr. Pinkerton has been
authorized to commence a new station on the Polela
River, about 200 miles inland. Additions to the churches
have been increasingly numerous, and the missionaries are
hopeful. One writes, in view of limited appropriations :
"We are not going backward; we shall 'go ahead'; and if
the American churches can't foot the bills, the Lord will."

There are now in this field 7 occupied stations, 14 out-
stations, 12 churches with 560 members, 4 native pastors,
9 native preachers, 18 catechists, 24 teachers, 830 pupils in
20 common schools, about 40 in a boys' boarding school at
Amanzimtote, and 9 in what may be called a theological
class rather than seminary. A female seminary at Inanda
has now 24 pupils and a girls' boarding school at Umzumbi is said to be very promising, with 14 pupils.

MISSIONARIES, 1876.	Went Out.	Station.
ZULU MISSION.		
Rev. David Rood	1847	Umvoti.
Mrs. Alzina V. Rood		
Rev. William Ireland	1848	Amanzimtote.
Mrs. R. O. Ireland		
Rev. Hyman A. Wilder	1849	Umtwalumi.
Mrs. Abby T. Wilder.		
Rev. Josiah Tyler	1849	Umsunduzi.
Mrs. Susan W. Tyler.		
Rev. Andrew Abraham	1849	Mapumulo.
Mrs. Sarah L. Abraham		
Rev. William Mellen	1851	Umsunduzi.
Mrs. Laurana W. Mellen	1851	
Rev. Stephen C. Pixley	1855	Inanda.
Mrs. Louisa Pixley	1855	
Rev. Elijah Robbins	1859	Amanzimtote.
Mrs. Addie B. Robbins	1859	
Rev. Henry M. Bridgman	1860	Umzumbi.
Mrs. Laura B. Bridgman	1860	
Mrs. Mary K. Edwards	1868	Inanda.
Miss Gertrude R. Hance	1870	Umvoti.
Miss Laura A. Day	1870	Amanzimtote.
Rev. Myron W. Pinkerton	1871	Umtwalumi.
Mrs. Laura M. Pinkerton	1871	
Miss Martha J. Lindley	1872	Inanda.
Rev. Charles W. Kilbon	1873	Inanda.
Mrs. Mary B. Kilbon	1873	
Miss Mary E. Pinkerton	1874	Umzumbi.

HISTORICAL SKETCH

OF THE

MISSIONS OF THE AMERICAN BOARD

IN

CHINA.

BY

Rev. S. C. BARTLETT, D. D.

BOSTON:

PUBLISHED BY THE BOARD,

1 Somerset Street.

1876.

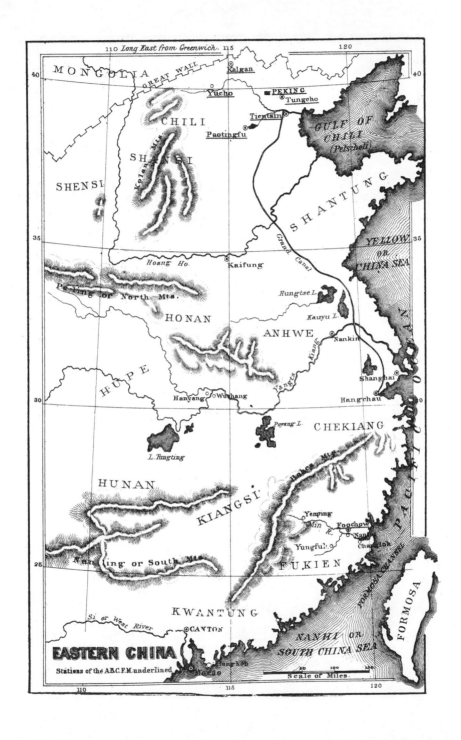

110 Long East from Greenwich 115   120

MONGOLIA

GREAT WALL

Kalgan

CHILI

Yucho

PEKING
Tungcho

Tientsin

Paotingfu

GULF OF
CHILI
(Petscheli)

SHANSI

SHENSI

Kolan Mts.

SHANTUNG

YELLOW
OR
CHINA SEA

Hoang Ho

Kaifung

Grand Canal

Peling or North Mts.

HONAN

Hungtse L.

Kauyu L.

ANHWE

Nankin

HUPE

Yangts Kiang

Shanghai

Hanyang Wuchang

Hangchau

CHEKIANG

Poyang L.

L. Tungting

HUNAN

KIANGSI

Bohea Mts.

Yenping

Min R. Foochow

Nan

Changchow

Yungful

Nanling or South Mts.

FUKIEN

FORMOSA CHANNEL

FORMOSA

KWANTUNG

Si or West River

CANTON

EASTERN CHINA

NANHI OR
SOUTH CHINA SEA

Hiangkoh

Stations of the A.B.C.F.M. underlined

Macao

Scale of Miles.

PACIFIC OCEAN

BARTLETT'S SKETCHES.

MISSIONS IN CHINA.

FEW minds comprehend the greatness of China, past, present, or prospective. When we utter those two short syllables, we mention one third of the human family; and each letter of that word stands for nearly a hundred million souls.

Every aspect of the empire is colossal. Huge mountain masses of immense altitude inclose it on the west, and shoot through the country their two long ranges so high that the great road from Canton to Pekin winds through a pass eight thousand feet above the ocean. Vast basins of land lying between and among these mountain ranges are fertilized and commercially interwoven by great navigable streams, the chief of which are the Hoang-ho, more than two thousand miles in length, and the Yang-tse Kiang, near three thousand miles long, ascended four hundred miles by the tide, and bearing myriads of barges and boats back and forth on its placid waters. Each of these, and other great rivers, are only the central threads of great networks of navigable streams, which render the empire pre-eminent among the nations in facilities for internal trade. Meanwhile the wide extent and varied surface of the country, stretching through thirty-eight degrees of latitude and seventy-four of longitude, give rise to almost every kind of climate, and admit

L

1

of almost every species of vegetable production ; and the numerous rivers are remarkable for the abundance and variety of their fish.   One tenth of the population derive their food from the waters.   Nature has bestowed on China certain peculiar treasures and sources of immense profit in the tea-plant, the camphor-tree, the sugar-cane, the bamboo, of endless uses, indigo, cotton, rhubarb, the varnish tree, and in the silk-worm, which is indigenous, and abounds in all parts of the country.   The mineral resources are ample — gold, silver, zinc, lead, and tin in considerable quantities, extensive mines of quicksilver, with iron and copper in great abundance.   Porcelain clay is found in great deposits, and immense stores of coal, bituminous and anthracite, and, in short, almost every mineral production requisite for the complete supply of the empire.   Not even our own country has an area more directly fitted and furnished by nature for a great concentric empire, with all its resources at home, than this grand Asiatic region.

In many respects the development of the empire has been proportionate to its resources.   The almost unequaled facilities for internal traffic afforded by its great river systems are increased by four hundred canals, greater in extent, possibly, than those of all other nations together, the longest of which was constructed six hundred years ago, and is twice the length of the Erie Canal.   The most titanic work of defense ever erected by man is that famous wall, from fifteen to thirty feet in height, fifteen feet broad at the top, and fifteen hundred miles in length, built so long ago that the centuries of its age are more by five than the hundreds of miles of its length.   The agriculture of China has been carried out on such a system as to utilize every kind and particle of refuse, and to maintain a density of population, in some of its provinces, — Kiang-ke, for example, — three times as great as the average of England, and more than twice that even of Belgium.

Those four or five hundred millions have been accumulating and toiling there for ages. *Old* England is an infant in the presence of China. Passing its fabulous era, the curtain of history rises two thousand years before Christ, and discloses already an elective monarchy; and the eye wearies with reading the names and the exact dates of fifty-eight monarchs, from Ta-yu to Yew-wang, who reigned on the Yang-tse Kiang before Romulus had sucked his " wolf's milk " on the banks of the Tiber. The empire boasts a hoary civilization too, which, if never quickened by the true religion, has yet accumulated splendid trophies. Its perfection of agriculture and its marvelous industry challenge our admiration. Many of its great canals are two thousand years old. From time immemorial the nation have been manufacturers of silks. Wood-engraving and stereotype printing are at least five hundred years older in China than the time of Gutenberg and Faust in Germany. The earliest Christian missionaries found here the magnetic needle. Gunpowder was in use at a remote antiquity, and the Tartars in the twelfth century learned here the use of guns and swords, and thence, perhaps, conveyed the knowledge of artillery to Europe. Seventeen hundred years ago the Chinese were using paper ; they had a lexicon of their language, that is still reckoned among their standards ; and the imperial library numbered eighty thousand volumes, two thirds of them " ancient " then.

One honorable mark of the pervasive civilization of China is found in the wide diffusion and high estimate

of education.   Distinction in public life can be attained
only on condition of scholarship, tested by rigid ex-
aminations.   The knowledge of reading, writing, and
arithmetic is with the men almost universal; so that
even the peasantry can keep their accounts, conduct their
correspondence, and read the proclamations of the mandarins.   In the southern provinces, especially, every
village has its school, founded and supported by the villages themselves.   To the foreign visitor the school-room
seems a young bedlam, for the children study rocking
themselves backward and forward, and chanting the
lesson, often indeed bawling it at the top of their voices.
In the midst of the hubbub sits the master, listening and
correcting; and when each pupil has thoroughly rocked
and screamed his lesson over to himself, he presents himself to the teacher with a low bow, and " backs his book,"
that is, he turns his back and repeats his lesson.   And it
marks the old and stereotyped character of the civilization, that the children learn largely the ancient writings
of Mencius and Confucius, committed in parrot style to
memory.   The peculiarities of the nation have been in-
tensified by its inner completeness and outward seclusion.
Shut off from the wave of western conquest by the
mountains of Thibet, enveloped by inhospitable plains on
the north, withdrawn from commerce by the breadth of
the Pacific, and intrenched within her own exclusive
policy, she knew for ages only the weaker nations and
roving tribes upon her borders.   Consequently, until
within these last few years the national conceit has been
insufferable and insuperable.   The emperor was the
"Son of Heaven," sitting on the "Dragon Throne,"
and signing decrees with the "vermilion pencil;" and
his empire was the "Middle Kingdom," the "Inner

Land," and the "Flowery Country." Their map of the world gave nine tenths of its space to China, and to England a spot as large as a thumb-nail, while our country was nowhere. The government documents designated foreigners as " barbarians," and the common people in many parts of the empire called them " foreign devils."

So diverse have been all their customs from our own, as to place a barrier between us from the outset. " We read horizontally, they perpendicularly ; and the columns run from right to left. We uncover the head as a mark of respect, they put on their caps. We black our boots, they whitewash them. We give the place of honor on the right, they on the left. We say the needle points to the north, they to the south. We shake the hand of a friend in salutation, they shake their own. We locate the understanding in the brain, they in the belly. We place our foot-notes at the bottom of the page, they at the top. In our libraries we set our books up, they lay theirs down. We now turn thousands of spindles and ply hundreds of shuttles without a single hand to propel, they employ a hand for each."

But the most singular thing of all, perhaps, is the language. Some have said it was specially invented by the devil to exclude Christianity. The fundamental conception of it is difficult for a foreigner to grasp. It is chiefly monosyllabic, having no other letters or words than syllables. In one respect it is as colossal as the nation — in the number of its characters. Every character is the name of a thing. An immense number of seemingly arbitrary signs is therefore to be mastered. The labor is alleviated, however, by the fact that there are certain root words, variously estimated at from three hundred and fifteen to four thousand, and some two hundred and fourteen symbolic characters, entering into, classifying, and characterizing the various combinations of signs. The number of words contained in the official dictionary is forty-three thousand five hundred, and other authorities reckon as many more. But the missionary Doolittle affirms that a knowledge of three or four thousand characters is sufficient for the reading of most books. The characters become so complicated in form that one remarkable specimen is made by fifty-two strokes of the pen. The language is still further complicated by the tones and inflections, which vary the meaning of the characters, and by the diversity of form and signification often attached to words identical in sound. The missionaries have found themselves greatly embarrassed, too, by the utter earthliness of the language. Among all its forty thousand words, rankly luxuriant in all the expressions for hateful passions and groveling vices, there was no suitable phraseology to describe one of the graces of the Spirit; and it was for half a century a matter of grave discussion what should be the proper name of God.

Difficult as the language confessedly is, the difficulty has, no doubt, been greatly magnified. It is one which for ages past has been constantly surmounted by these countless millions themselves; it is one which Dr. Milne overcame so readily as to publish an address in Chinese within a twelvemonth after he entered the field. And the labor of acquisition is more than counterbalanced by the breadth of utterance. For though there are numerous spoken dialects, mutually unintelligible, the written language of this vast empire is one. And the weary translator, toiling at his task, may cheer himself with the thought that every verse he painfully prepares can speak in God's name to any one of four hundred million souls.

The labor was lightened, too, from the beginning, by the fact that the missionary needed no outlay for types, presses, and printing offices with foreign printers and binders, but had only to give his manuscript to a Chinaman, and receive back his book all printed, and bound, and ready for circulation.

China has been called the Gibraltar of heathenism. In some respects the statement is true. The complication of the language is, after all, but a trivial barrier, for it can be as well surmounted for the cause of Christ as for every earthly purpose. We long had a grand obstacle in the overweening vanity and singular exclusiveness of the nation; but the collisions with England and France, twelve years ago, have shaken these to their centre. There still remains the wonderful tenacity with which the nation identifies itself with the past and clings to its time-honored institutions, and especially the mighty hold which Confucius has upon their reverence and actual adoration. Considering the number of centuries since his death — twenty-three — and the multitudes of men who have ever since chosen him for their great light, no man has ever carried so wide an influence. Said two old men of Shantung, refusing a religious tract, "We have seen your books, and do not want them. In the instructions of our sage we have sufficient." They only gave voice to the hereditary feeling. Those doctrines, at their best estate, are but a self-sufficient morality. Another powerful obstacle to the true religion is the worship paid to deceased ancestors. It has its regular services and set times in every household; is established by universal custom, compulsory by public sentiment, and, if neglected, enforceable by law. When we consider how deep are the sentiments of human nature on which it lays hold, we can easily see how firm that hold must be. The nation is also trained from childhood to the practice of innumerable other idolatrous ceremonies, till they have become a network in which the whole life is woven. These idolatries are supported at enormous expense. A missionary who had made careful inquiry through the district of Shanghai, and estimated the empire on the same scale, computed the annual expenditures of Chinese idolatry at the almost increditable sum of one hundred and eighty millions of dollars. Surely there is some money-power in China arrayed against the annual half a million of the American Board, expended on the world.

But perhaps neither Confucianism, Tauism, nor Buddhism, — the three chief forms of religion, — offer obstacles so great as the character and habits of the nation. Under a calm and courteous exterior, foreigners have found them cunning and corrupt, treacherous and vindictive. Gambling and drunkenness, though abundantly prevalent, are far outstripped by their licentiousness, which taints the language with its leprosy, often decorates the walls of their inns with the foulest of scenes, by them called " flowers," and lurks beneath a thin Chinese lacker as a deep dead-rot in society. Said Dr. Bridgman, after sixteen years' labor among them, — and Mr. Johnson, with a still longer experience, confirmed his words, — " The longer I live in this country, the more do I see of the wickedness of this people. All that Paul said of the ancient heathen is true of the Chinese, and true to an extent that is dreadful. Their inmost soul, their very conscience, seems to be seared, dead — so insensible that they are, as regards a future life, like the beasts that perish. No painting, no imagination, can portray and lay before the Christian world the awful sins, the horrible abominations, that fill the land."

Associated with all this corruption is the deepest degradation of woman. From the cradle to the grave her life is one long-drawn woe. Her birth is a disgrace and a burden to the family ; and infanticide of females accordingly prevails to a shocking extent. In forty towns around Amoy, Mr. Abeel found that two fifths of the girls were destroyed in their infancy ; and intelligent Chinese informed Mr. Doolittle that probably more than half the families of the great city of Foo Chow have destroyed one or more of their daughters — drowned in tubs, thrown into streams, and buried alive, commonly by the father. Sometimes they are exposed, sometimes sold in infancy for slaves or for wives. A girl of one year will bring two dollars, and each additional year, till she is old enough to work and be more valuable, two dollars more. If spared alive at home, she is but a menial ; taught to work, but not to read or write. She is sold in marriage to some man whom she never sees till the wedding day — a man with whom she never eats, who holds and uses the right to starve her, beat her, or to sell her permanently or transiently to some other man, or in due time to place another wife by her side. From the prolonged curse of life not seldom she escapes by suicide. Said the Mandarin Ting to the French traveler Huc, folding his arms, and stepping back a pace or two, " Women have no souls." And when it was insisted and argued that they had, he laughed long and loud at the thought. " When I get home I will tell my wife she has a soul. She will be astonished, I think." Does not one mighty wail sweep over the waters of the Pacific, and sound day and night in the ears of the wives, mothers, and daughters of this country, beseeching them to go and to send to the rescue of these their degraded, suffering sisters ?

One other obstacle only shall be mentioned — the use of opium. Perhaps it is the most formidable of all. Two names deserve to be handed down to infamy : those of Vice-President Wheeler and Colonel Watson, of the British East India Company, who, in the beginning of this century, conceived the deplorable thought of sending the opium of Bengal into China. Even the heathen empire roused itself at length, and nobly struggled hard to eject the horrid gift, — this Pandora's box, — but the British government, in 1840, forced it back at the cannon's mouth. The effect has been hideous beyond description. The physical, social, and moral evils with which it is steadily flooding the nation, in its lava-like course, no tongue can tell. The Chinese grow excited when they speak of it ; and the missionaries, with one voice, declare it to be, next to native depravity, the most dreadful barrier to the progress of the gospel. Surely Christendom owes China the gospel with a fearful force of obligation.

No doubt the difficulties are great. But the motive, and the moving power, are greater far. Here is a huge prize for the Lord of Hosts. If China has been thought the Gibraltar, it may yet become the Waterloo, of heathendom. Long ago Christian eyes were turned to the shining mark. Twelve centuries ago the Nestorian Church, in her palmy days, planted churches in China, which, after various successes and reverses, were crushed by the heel of Genghis Khan, overrun by the victorious march of the Mohammedan princes, and forcibly obliterated by the dynasty of Ming. In the thirteenth century Rome came here with an archbishop, seven assistant bishops, and a train of missionaries. Again she returned in 1581, in Jesuit disguise, led by one Ricci, of whom a

Catholic writer thus speaks : " The kings found in him a man full of complaisance ; the pagans a minister who accommodated himself to their superstitions ; the Mandarins a polite courtier, skilled in all the courts ; and the devil a faithful servant, who, far from destroying, established his reign among the people, and even extended it to the Christians." Since that time, by the customary superficial methods, which in China do not include the distribution of the Scriptures, and very seldom the ability to preach intelligibly, the Papacy has prosecuted its work, till in China proper it now boasts of twenty bishops, four hundred and seventy priests (half of them natives), and three hundred and sixty thousand converts, or baptized persons.

The father of Protestant missions in China was Rev. Robert Morrison — a man who had prepared for the Divinity School, at Hoxton, by studying between the hours of seven at night and six in the morning, making boot-trees during the day. With a burning desire to preach to the heathen, he broke away from the dissuasions of his friends and the tears of his father, to this dark land. Under the charge of the London Missionary Society, and with a letter from James Madison to the American Consul at Canton, he, in 1807, found his way in that city to the ware-rooms of a New York merchant, where, in the native costume, with long nails and cue, he ate, slept, lived, and studied by day, and, with his small brown earthen lamp, by night, praying his daily prayers in broken Chinese. After seven long years, he gave the natives the New Testament entire, and baptized his first convert from a little spring gushing from the hill-side by the sea, in utter solitude. In that same year he was joined by the noble William Milne, who had

sprung from a Scotch peasant's home ; at the age of sixteen had spent whole evenings at prayer in a sheep-cote,
kneeling on a bit of turf that he carried with him ; at
twenty had consecrated himself to the mission work ;
then spent five years in providing for his sisters and
widowed mother ; told the committee-man, who objected
to his rustic appearance, that he was ready to go as a
hewer of wood and a drawer of water, so that he might
be in the work, and in a year from his arrival was publishing a Chinese address.   Three years later, Morrison
and Milne issued the whole of the Scriptures, — a work
which, in her hundreds of years of occupancy, the Romish Church never did nor attempted.   Other translations
have since been published, — the New Testament, in
Mandarin colloquial, quite recently, at Peking.   Morrison
and Milne were feebly reënforced from home, and after
almost a quarter of a century, their earnest call — which
proved to be Milne's dying call — reached America.   It
was then (1829) that the American Board began its work
in the persons of the excellent Bridgman and Abeel, followed in succession by other noble men and women, some
of whom have also followed them to heaven, in firm faith
of the sure harvest in due season.   Among earlier members of the mission were Williams, Parker, Doty, Pohl-
man, Ball, Peet, Bonney, and other honored names.   The
Board is at present * represented in China by thirty-nine
Americans, male and female, who, with their native
preachers and helpers, occupy some seven stations, and
fifteen out-stations, where they have organized eleven
small churches.   Other Protestant Boards have followed
them, until, according to a recent statement prepared at
Tientsin, one hundred and twenty-four [ordained] missionaries are now in the field, who, with their wives,

* 1872.

other helpers, and native preachers and assistants, occupy some twenty-six principal points and adjacent stations. Morrison's, Marshman's, Gutzlaff's, and Medhurst's translations of the Bible, and other versions, or partial versions, have been issued, together with some eight hundred different tracts and books, many of which have been widely circulated. Many churches have been organized; most of them small, although three of those belonging to the Reformed Church at Amoy together number three hundred and seventy-seven communicants. Already native pastors are at the head of some of these churches, while many native evangelists are preaching the gospel to their countrymen. The number of converts was given, two years ago, by Mr. Williams, Secretary of Legation at Peking, as several thousand.

But the history of missions in China is a history still of the future; let us hope of the near future, and a glorious history. For " what are these among so many" — one missionary to three or four millions of people? They stand oppressed before the greatness of the work, and the magnificence of the opportunity, amid the wonderful *renaissance* that is sweeping over China. Mr. Chapin wrote from Tientsin, in 1867: "Would that we had a hundred men full of faith, and zeal, and love. Where is there such a field? I wonder that the hearts of the pious and enterprising youth of our country are not so stirred up, in view of the glorious service, as to lead thousands of them to present themselves to the Board, and beg to be sent forth on this holy, joyous mission."

It is, indeed, a future of glorious hope and possibilities. Great as are the obstacles, the power of the gospel has shown itself greater, and some of the very obstacles may

M

yet throw their enormous weight upon its side. The Holy Spirit has proved his ability to pierce the worldly and sensual Chinese heart.

Tsae A-ke, that first convert whom Morrison baptized in the solitude of the sea-shore, proved faithful unto death, and many others have proved, also, faithful in life, till now that solitary believer is represented by several thousand, many of whom are faithful preachers of the word. The Missionary Herald recently informed us of a young Chinese merchant in Hawaii, who has left his business to labor for Christ among his countrymen upon those islands. A gentleman in manner and character, he speaks English, Hawaiian, and six dialects of the Chinese, and preaches with fervor and with power; and his countrymen there are abandoning their idolatry, and predicting the speedy prevalence of Christianity through their native empire.

God has, indeed, wrought wonders since that time, — not a generation gone by, — when the whole foreign intercourse of the empire was concentrated in the Hong merchants of Canton. The opium war closed, in 1842, by unlocking five other ports to open commerce. The war with France and England, ending in 1860, did still greater things. It reversed the policy of the empire. When the foreign armies steadily advanced toward Peking, storming every fort on the way till they had burned the summer palace, and invested the capital, the treacherous Emperor fled to Tartary, the national vanity and obstinacy broke down together, and a new day dawned on China. Not only are eighteen ports now open to trade, but the empire is free to foreign travel and teaching, with the definite pledge of toleration to Christianity, and of protection to its missionaries. The government has at length learned, by hard experience, thoroughly to respect and desire the civilization of the West. Chinese troops have been drilled in foreign tactics on the very battle-grounds where they had been defeated within the year. The Viceroy of the Fukien and Chekiang provinces is building gun-boats by the aid of French ship-builders, and is training thirty young men to learn the French language and the art of ship-building, and as many more to learn the English and the art of navigation. Wheaton's Law of Nations has, by order of the government, been translated and distributed to the officials of the empire ; and so well has it been conned, that, in a recent difficulty of the Prussian Minister with the authorities, he was both astounded and discomfited by their citation of its principles. The government has founded the University of Peking. There is a longing for foreign science, so earnest that it will suffer the leaven of Christianity that accompanies, as when the Viceroy of Kiangnan publishes, with his own sanction and introduction, a translation of Euclid, wherein the missionary translator boldly advocates the cause of religion in the preface. A man of wealth and learning has recently argued, in one of the Chinese papers, in favor of the missionary work as a matter of policy, declaring that " the benefits which we derive from the teachings of the missionaries are more than we can enumerate," and that " their influence on our future will be unbounded." The embassy of Mr. Burlingame was a startling event in the drowsy policy of this ancient empire. A powerful progressive party is rising into influence which may yet throw the momentum of the empire in favor of Christianity. For it seems an admitted fact — reiterated to Mr. Burlingame by a member of the Board of Foreign Affairs — that the intelligent men of China "put no faith in the popular religions," and that a large part of the people, notwithstanding their industrious observances of forms, are wholly indifferent to the principles of their faith. Thousands of copies of the Bible, and other Christian books and tracts, have been scattered among this reading people. They begin to ask for Christian books. Attention is turned to Christianity. Mr. Lees, of the London Society, and Mr. Williamson, of the Scotch Bible Society, in an extended tour in 1866, found many who bought their books, and hung eagerly on their words. Mr. Chapin, in his journeys in the neighborhood of Tientsin, spoke to audiences of two or three thousand persons. Mr. Williamson, of the Bible Society, after a two months' tour from Peking, reported the people as calling for the living preacher. The very degradation of the Chinese women may yet prodigiously react in behalf of our religion, with its elevation of the sex. The girls' schools are already growing in favor. Mr. Williams writes from Peking that they are specially encouraged by their access to the women, who in several families welcome their visits; and Mr. Blodget speaks of "boat loads of women" coming in from the country towns, bringing their food with them, to be instructed in the gospel. Mrs. Gulick, on her visit to Yücho, while talking to a room full of women, was accosted by one who took her by the hand, saying, "I believe in Jesus, and last New Year's day burned all my idols." Others were much moved; three or four offered simple, but earnest prayers, declared their faith in Jesus, and asked for baptism.

In truth, the long dormant elements in China are rousing to action. A period of awakening, and of possible instruction, has come at last. It is a time of formation and of hope. Everything is ready and waiting. It is an important hour for that vast empire. Where, now, is the solid phalanx of young Christian heroes, wise with a heavenly wisdom, fired with a Christ-like zeal, and filled with a largeness of heart, and a breadth of comprehension, as great as the opportunity, to cast themselves into the breach, and win the empire to Christ? Where are those men? Let them now stand forth, unfurl the banner of the cross, and call on the churches to pour out their prayers and their money like water for their support. And the churches dare not say them nay. China and the world will owe them the profoundest debt of gratitude, and the Master will say, " Well done." Has there been such an opportunity since the world began?

While preparing this article for the press the writer has met with a statement which casts new light on the prospects and condition of China, and more than confirms all the foregoing assertions. It shows how great a foundation has been laid, and how rapidly the work rolls up, increasing as it goes. It shows, also, how firm a hold the gospel can lay upon the seemingly wooden heart and mind of the Chinaman. It was written by Rev. S. L. Baldwin, a Methodist Episcopal missionary, and appeared in the Independent, December 21, 1871, in answer to certain disparaging inquiries of a contributor. It is a pretty effectual answer : —

" I. What has been accomplished in China?

" *Answer*. — Although the first Protestant missionary to the Chinese landed at Canton in 1807, and about sixty missionaries were sent from Europe and America, between 1813 and 1842, to China, and to the Chinese settlements in Java, Siam, and the Straits, the real era of the commencement of Protestant missionary labor in China is the year 1842, in which the treaty with Great Britain was signed, which opened the ' five ports ' to the commerce of the world. Our missionaries were then permitted to enter at all the open ports with the word of life. A long period of preparatory work was then entered upon — breaking down the prejudices of a people for centuries secluded from the rest of the world, overcoming the superstitions of the masses, and undermining their faith in idolatry. While this work was going on — for ten or twelve years — there were scarcly any converts ; so that nearly all the converts have been received within the last sixteen years, and by far the larger part of them within the last seven years. The following table will show the ratio of increase during the last eighteen years :—

In 1853 the number of native Christians was . . 351
" 1863   "   "   "   "   . . 1,974
" 1864   "   "   "   "   . . 2,607
" 1868   "   "   "   "   . . 5,743
The present number is very nearly 8,000

" But we should get a very inadequate idea of the work done if we were to look only at the number of communicants. Over five hundred different books have been printed in the Chinese language by Protestant missionaries, including the Sacred Scriptures, commentaries, theological, educational, linguistic, historical, geographical, mathematical, astronomical, and botanical works — books ranging in size and importance from the child's primer to Dr. Martin's translation of ' Wheaton's International Law,' Dr. Hobson's medical and physiological works, and Mr. Wylie's translations of ' Euclid's Geometry ' and ' Herschell's Astronomy.'

" Besides, the vast advance made in eradicating the prejudices of the people, securing their confidence, and gaining entrance into the interior, is to be taken into the account. The fact that fifty thousand native patients are annually treated in Protestant missionary hospitals is also full of significance. It is a common thing for us to meet with people now who say that for eight, or ten, or more years they have not worshiped idols ; that they were convinced by preaching that they heard, or books that they received, so long ago, that idolatry was wrong, and had given it up. We find them now, in interior cities and villages, ready to become adherents of the gospel of Christ.

" II.   What are our prospects for the future ?

" *Answer.* — Rev. M. J. Knowlton, of Ningpo, calls attention to the fact that of late the number of out-stations, of native preachers, and of converts has doubled once in a period of a little over three years, and that we may reasonably expect that by the year 1900 the native Christians will number over two millions.   Bishop Kingsley, in addressing the native Methodist preachers at Foochow, in 1869, reminded them that there were more Methodists then in Foochow than there were in America a hundred years before.   Let this fact be borne in mind, namely, that, although the Chinese move slowly, when they begin to move they move in masses, and there is no reason why this rule may not operate to the advantage of Christianity.   In the Foochow mission of the Methodist Episcopal church we had last year nine hundred and thirty-one members, and nine hundred and sixty-nine probationers, showing the work of the year preceding to have equaled, in the number of converts, all the years of the mission's history that had gone before.

Such facts as these will have weight with all thinking minds.

"III. What is the character of Chinese converts?

"*Answer.* — As among converts at home, there is every variety of character among them; but in general they are faithful, earnest, devoted men. The difference between them and their Pagan neighbors is marked. The Pagan neighbor is dirty. The Christian is clean. The Pagan lies, and delights in lying. The Christian becomes truthful. The Pagan treats his wife as a slave. The Christian treats her as an immortal being. The Pagan regards the birth of a daughter as a calamity. The Christian welcomes the little girl, gives her to God in baptism, and tries to prepare her for a useful life.

"One of our native Christians at Foochow went on Saturday to an American mercantile house with samples of tea. The agent in charge said, 'Come to-morrow.' The native replied, 'To-morrow is Sunday, and I never transact business on God's day!' (Some incidents of this kind may go far to account for the asserted fact that 'merchants do not expect great things from the missionaries.')

"When Li Cha Mi, a few weeks ago, was stoned by persecutors until he was nearly dead, and afterward, in attempting to elude his pursuers, fell over a precipice twenty feet high, while he was falling he prayed, 'Lord, have mercy upon them, and forgive them.'

"After Ling Ching Ting had been beaten with two thousand stripes, as soon as he was able to move he returned to the place where he had been beaten, and preached the gospel so faithfully that some of the very men who brought that trial upon him were converted.

"When Hii Yong Mi was driven from his home by a

mob, and his wife cruelly outraged, they both held stead-fast to their faith in Christ, emulating the spirit of Job : ' Though he slay me, yet will I trust in him.'

" When old Father Ling, at Ku-cheng, was told by heathen friends, ' You must not try to give up opium smoking now after forty years' practice ; it will kill you ; ' his reply was, ' I belong to Jesus. I have prom-ised to give up every sin. I would rather die trying to conquer this sin than live an opium smoker.'

" I speak only of men I have personally known, whose Christian character commands my admiration, and whose Christian lives are evidence of the genuineness of their profession."

March, 1876.

A new edition of this sketch being now called for, it may be well, without changing the stereotype plates of the foregoing pages, to append a few sentences, bringing the statistics of existing missions of the American Board down to the present time. The missions are the same as in 1871, but some changes have taken place in the mission force.

Rev. J. E. Walker, and Miss Claghorn, now Mrs. Walker, joined the *Foochow mission* in 1872, and Rev. J. B. Blakely and wife in 1874. Mr. and Mrs. Peet have retired from the work. In 1873 this mission made an earnest effort, with the coöperation of native helpers, to extend its work to the northwestern part of the province, up the Min River, and succeeded in renting places and locating helpers at Yang-kau, one hundred and eighty miles from Foochow, and at Tsiang-loh, forty miles beyond Yang-kau. Considerable success has attended the labors of the helpers there and of the missionaries, as they have been able to visit the region, and the brethren hope to find many openings and ere long to have a station in that vicinity occupied by American missionaries. There are now eleven small churches, — at the two stations and nine (of the seventeen) outstations of this mission, — with a total membership of 163. Twenty-five members were received during the last year reported, and the condition of the churches is spoken of as quite encouraging. Miss Payson has had charge, for some years, of a boarding-school for girls, which reports twenty-four pupils, and there is a small training school for young men, under Mr. Baldwin's care, where some of those already employed as helpers, and others, receive instruction with a view to their greater usefulness as teachers, preachers, and pastors. Seventeen of the thirty-three native helpers in the mission work are now reported as "preachers." Dr. Osgood's medical work has been one of growing prosperity and usefulness. The number of patients treated during the last year reported was about six thousand. The latest report of the mission represents the work as quite hopeful when compared with the past, though the field is still felt to be one not easy of cultivation and not promising large immediate results.

The *North China mission* has been reinforced since 1871 as follows : Rev. Arthur H. Smith and wife, Rev. Henry D. Porter, M. D., and Miss Jane G. Evans, went out in 1872 ; Rev. M. W. Hunt and wife in 1873 ; and Rev. Wm. P. Sprague and wife in 1874. The stations of the mission are six : Tientsin, Peking, Kalgan, Tung-cho, Yü-cho and Pao-ting-fu ; with seven churches — two at Peking and one at each of the other stations — and a total of 171 members. Thirty-six were added by profession during the last year reported. The native helpers in this field are few

as yet, — six " catechists " and three other helpers. There
is a training-school at Tung-cho with "station classes"
at other points, but the number of young men under instruction is not large. Other schools also are small, but
some of them — especially the Female Seminary, called
the Bridgman School, at Peking, under the care of Misses
Porter and Chapin — not without promise of much usefulness. Earnest efforts are made among women by the
ladies of the mission ; medical work is much called for ;
something has been done towards extending the influence
and labors of the mission into Mongolia ; from the press,
in charge of Mr. P. R. Hunt, 2,900,000 pages were issued
within the last year reported, but there is a very limited
interest among the Chinese in foreign books. The last
report of the mission states : "The hindrances that re-
tard and embarrass us remain as heretofore. They are,
in general, the *inertia* of the people, the power of present superstitions, ignorance, conceit, timidity, sordidness,
and spiritual bondage in sin. These things combine to
make the people prejudiced and suspicious. The encour-
agements are the continued peaceful occupation of the
present places of labor, and a growing measure of good-
will on the part of the people toward the missionaries, as
they learn more of their character and of Christian doctrines. The door for the proclamation of the gospel is
fairly opened.

MISSIONARIES, 1876.	Went Out.	Station.
FOOCHOW MISSION.		
Rev. C. C. Baldwin, D. D.	1847	Foochow.
Mrs Harriet F. Baldwin	1847	
Rev. Charles Hartwell	1852	Nantai.
Mrs. Lucy E. Hartwell	1852	
Rev. Simeon F. Woodin	1859	Nantai.
Mrs. Sarah L. Woodin	1859	
Miss Adelia M. Payson	1868	Nantai.
D. W. Osgood, M. D.	1869	Nantai.
Mrs. Helen W. Osgood	1869	
Rev. J. E. Walker	1872	Foochow.
Mrs. E. A. Walker	1872	
Rev. J. B. Blakely	1874	Foochow.
Mrs. Isabella Blakely	1874	
MISSION TO NORTH CHINA.		
Rev. Henry Blodget, D. D.	1854	Peking.
Mrs. Sarah F. R. Blodget	1854	
Rev. C. A. Stanley	1862	Tientsin.
Mrs. Ursula Stanley	1862	
Rev. Lyman D. Chapin	1862	Tung-cho.
Mrs. Clara L. Chapin	1862	
Rev. Chauncey Goodrich	1865	Tung-cho.
Rev. John T. Gulick	1864	Kalgan.
Rev. Mark Williams	1866	Kalgan.
Mrs. Isabella B. Williams	1866	
Alfred O. Treat, M. D.	1867	Pao-ting-fu.
Phineas R. Hunt	1868	Peking.
Mrs. Abigail N. Hunt	1868	
Miss M. E. Andrews	1868	Tung-cho.
Miss Mary H. Porter	1868	Peking.
Rev. Thomas W. Thompson . . .	1868	Kalgan.
Rev. Chester Holcombe	1869	Peking.
Mrs. Olive K. Holcombe	1869	
Rev. Devello Z. Sheffield	1869	Tung-cho.
Mrs. Eleanor W. Sheffield	1869	
Miss Naomi Diament	1870	Kalgan.
Rev. Isaac Pierson	1870	Pao-ting-fu.
Miss Jennie E. Chapin	1871	Peking.
Rev. Henry D. Porter, M. D. . . .	1872	Tientsin.
Rev. Arthur H. Smith	1872	Tientsin.
Mrs. Emma J. Smith	1872	Tientsin.
Miss Jennie G. Evans	1872	Tung-cho.
Rev. Myron W. Hunt	1873	Pao-ting-fu.
Mrs. Laura A. Hunt	1873	
Rev. William P. Sprague	1874	Kalgan.
Mrs. Margaret S. Sprague	1874	

HISTORICAL SKETCH

OF THE

MISSIONS OF THE AMERICAN BOARD

IN

INDIA AND CEYLON.

BY

REV. S. C. BARTLETT, D. D.

BOSTON:
PUBLISHED BY THE BOARD,
1 SOMERSET STREET.
1876.

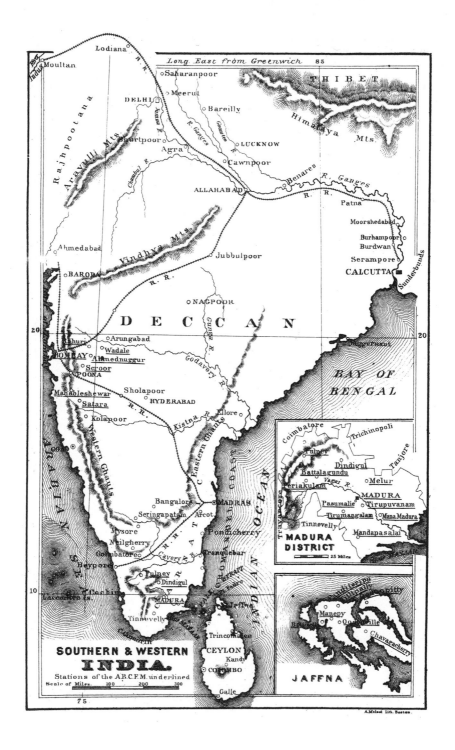

SOUTHERN & WESTERN
INDIA.
Stations of the A.B.C.F.M. underlined
Scale of Miles. 100   200   300

A.Meisel Lith. Boston.

BARTLETT'S SKETCHES.

MISSIONS IN INDIA AND CEYLON.

HENRY MARTYN knew the Hindoos well; and he once said, " If ever I see a Hindoo a real believer in Jesus, I shall see something more nearly approaching the resurrection of a dead body than anything I have yet seen."

But God knows how to raise the dead. And it was on this most hopeless race, under the most discouraging concurrence of circumstances, that he chose to let the first missionaries of the American Board try their fresh zeal.

The movements of commerce and the history of previous missionary effort naturally pointed to the swarming continent of Asia. It was over this benighted region that Mills brooded at his studies. The British Baptist mission near Calcutta readily suggested the particular field of India, and the impression was deepened by the ardent imagination of young Judson. His mind had, in 1809, been so " set on fire " by a moderate sermon of Buchanan's, the " Star of the East," that for some days he was unable to attend to the studies of the class; and at a later period, a now forgotten book, Colonel Symes's " Embassy to Ava," full of glowing and overwrought descriptions, stirred him with a fascination for Burmah which he never lost. The Prudential Committee of the Board also looked to the Burman Empire because it was

beyond the control of British authority, and therefore beyond "the proper province of the British Missionary
Society."

Judson did indeed find his way to Burmah, but in a
mode how different from what he expected! cut adrift
from his associates, and fleeing from British authority.
The Board established this mission, but in a place and
with a history how diverse from their intentions! Man
proposes, but God disposes. Bombay became the first
missionary station.

And that choice band of young disciples — God had
roused their several hearts, brought them together from
their distant homes, and united their burning zeal, to
scatter them in the opening of their labor. There was
Mills, given to God by his mother, now strengthening
her faltering resolution; there was Hall, ready to work
his passage, and throw himself on God's providence, in
order to preach the gospel to the heathen; there was
Judson, ardent, bold, and strong; and Newell, humble,
tender, and devoted; there was Nott, with the deep
"sense of a duty to be done;" and Rice, whose earnest
desire to join the mission the Committee "did not dare
to reject;" and there was the noble Ann Hasseltine, with
a heart all alive with missionary zeal before the Lord
brought Judson to her father's house in Bradford, and
the young Harriet Atwood, gentle, and winning, and firm,
mourning at the age of seventeen over the condition of
the heathen, and at eighteen joining heart and hand with
Newell, to carry them the gospel. Of all this precious
band, two only, Hall and Newell, did God permit to bear
a permanent part in that projected mission. Mills was
to die on mid-ocean, in the service of Africa; Harriet
Newell was to pass away before she found a resting-

place for the sole of her foot; Nott was to break down with the first year's experience of the climate; Mr. and Mrs. Judson, and Mr. Rice, were to found another great missionary enterprise.

On the 19th of February, 1812, the Caravan sailed from Salem, with Judson, and Newell, and their wives on board; and on the 20th, the Harmony, from Philadelphia, with Nott, and Hall, and Rice; the one vessel going forth from the heart of Congregationalism, the other from the centre of Presbyterianism, carrying the sympathies of both denominations. They sailed through the midst of the embargo and non-intercourse; and the note of war with England followed their track upon the waters.

Their instructions pointed them to the Burman Empire, but gave them discretionary power to go elsewhere. The Burman Empire could be reached only through the British possessions, and both vessels were accordingly bound for Calcutta. But the British authorities in India at that time were resolutely opposed to Christian missions. The East India Company professed to believe that the preaching of the gospel would excite the Hindoos to rebellion, and was meanwhile drawing a large revenue from the protection of idolatry. The Baptist missionaries at Serampore had felt the power of this hostility, but, being British subjects, and having long held the ground, could not be dispossessed.

But the spirit of hostility had of late been kindled up anew. In the very year when Mills and Rice were founding their secret missionary society at Williams College, Rev. Sydney Smith was stirring up the British public, through the enginery of the Edinburgh Review, against the British mission in India. He opened by

insinuating that the mutiny at Vellore was connected
with a recent increase of the missionary force; he continued with ridicule of " Brother Carey's " and " Brother
Thomas' " Journals, and closed with an elaborate argument to show the folly of founding missions in India. He
argues, first, from the danger of insurrection; secondly,
from " want of success," the effort being attended with
difficulties which he seems to think " insuperable; "
thirdly, from " the exposure of the converts to great
present misery; " and fourthly, he declares conversion to
be " no duty at all if it merely destroys the old religion,
without really and effectually teaching the new one." In
regard to the last point, he argues that making a Christian is only destroying a Hindoo, and remarks that " after
all that has been said of the vices of the Hindoos, we believe that a Hindoo is more mild and sober than most
Europeans, and as honest and chaste." Such was the tone
of feeling he represented, and he returned next year to
the task of " routing out " " a nest of consecrated cob-
blers." The Baptist missionaries are " ferocious Methodists " and " impious coxcombs," and when they complain of intolerance, " a weasel might as well complain
of intolerance when it is throttled for sucking eggs." He
declares that the danger of losing the East India possessions " makes the argument against them conclusive, and
shuts up the case; " and he adds, that " our opinion of
the missionaries and of their employers is such that we
most firmly believe, in less than twenty years, for the
conversion of a few degraded wretches, who would be
neither Methodists nor Hindoos, they would infallibly
produce the massacre of every European in India." To
this hostile feeling towards missionaries in general was

soon added the weight of open warfare between England and America.

The Caravan reached her destination on the 17th of June. Scarcely had the first warm greetings of Christian friends been uttered, when the long series of almost apostolic trials began. Ten days brought an order from government, commanding the return of the missionaries in the Caravan. They asked leave to reside in some other part of India, but were forbidden to settle in any part of the Company's territory, or its dependencies. May they not go to the Isle of France? It was granted. And Mr. and Mrs. Newell took passage in the first vessel, leaving their comrades, for whom there was no room on board. Four days later arrived the Harmony; and Hall, Nott, and Rice also were summoned before the police, and ordered to return in the same vessel. They also applied for permission to go to the Isle of France; and while waiting for the opportunity, another most "trying event" befell them. Mr. and Mrs. Judson, after many weeks of hidden but conscientious investigation, changed their views, and joined the Baptists. Four weeks later and another shock; Mr. Rice had followed Judson. "What the Lord means," wrote Hall and Nott, "by thus dividing us in sentiment and separating us from each other, we cannot tell." But we can now tell, that the Lord meant another great missionary enterprise, with more than a hundred churches and many thousand converts in the Burman Empire.

While the brethren still waited, they gained favorable intelligence of Bombay, and especially of its new governor. They received a general passport to leave in the ship Commerce, paid their passage, and got their trunks aboard, when there came a peremptory order to proceed

C

in one of the Company's ships to England, and their names were published in the list of passengers. They, however, used their passports, and embarked for Bombay, while the police made a show of searching the city for them, but did not come near the vessel. In a twelve-month from the time of their ordination, they reached Bombay, to be met there by a government order to send them to England.

While the Commerce was carrying Hall and Nott to Bombay, another sad blow was preparing. Harriet Newell was dying of quick consumption at the Isle of France. Peacefully, and even joyfully, she passed away, sending messages of the tenderest love to her distant relatives, comforting her heart-broken husband, and exhibiting a faith serene and unclouded. "Tell them [my dear brothers and sisters], and also my dear mother, that I have never regretted leaving my native land for the cause of Christ." "I wish to do something for God before I die. But . . . I long to be perfectly free from sin. God has called me away before we have entered on the work of the mission, but the case of David affords me comfort. I have had it in my heart to do what I can for the heathen, and I hope God will accept me." She is told she can not live through the day. "O, joyful news! I long to depart." And so she departed, calling, with faltering speech, "My dear Mr. Newell, my husband," and ending her utterance on earth with, "How long, O Lord, how long?" And yet God turned this seeming calamity into an unspeakable blessing. Mr. Nott, half a century later, well recounts it as one of the "providential and gracious aids to the establishment of the first foreign mission," and remembers "its influence on our minds in strengthening our missionary purposes."

And not only so, but the tale of her youthful consecration, and her faith and purpose, unfaltering in death, thrilled through the land. How many eyes have wept over the touching narrative, and how many hearts have throbbed with kindred resolutions ! " No long-protracted life could have so blessed the church as her early death." Look at one instance. The little town of Smyrna lies on the Chenango River in central New York. It had neither church, minister, nor Sabbath school; and never had witnessed a revival of religion. The Memoir of Harriet Newell, dropped into one woman's hands in that town, began a revival of religion in her heart, through her house, through that town, and through that region. Two evangelical churches grew out of that revival. Men and women who were born again at that time, have carried far and wide the power of the cross and the institutions of the gospel. On the Isle of France there still is seen a stranger's grave, while another solitary tomb may be seen on the distant Island of St. Helena. The one formerly contained the world's great Captain, the other holds the ashes of a missionary girl. But how infinitely nobler that woman's life and influence !

From February till December, Hall and Nott, at Bombay, were kept in suspense, and even in expectation of defeat. The Governor of that Presidency was personally friendly, but overborne by his official instructions. Twice were they directed to return in the next vessel, their names being once entered on the list of passengers, and at another time their baggage being made ready for the ship, and the Coolies waiting to take it. Again and again were they told there was no alternative, till all hope had passed. Hall had made his final appeal, in a letter of almost Pauline boldness and courtesy, in which he bade

the Governor " Adieu, till we meet you face to face at
God's tribunal." The very next day they were informed
that they might remain till further instructions were received; and in due time they gained full permission to
labor in any part of the Presidency. The Company had
yielded to the powerful influence brought to bear, not only
from without, but from within their own body at home.
When, at the last moment, the Court of Directors were
on the point of enforcing their policy, a powerful argument from Sir Charles Grant, founded on the documents
of the missionaries, turned the scale. *India was open.*

Hall and Nott were soon joined by Newell, who, bereft
as he was, and for a time supposing that his comrades
had all been sent back, had yet resolved to labor alone
in Ceylon.

Bombay thus became the Plymouth of the American
mission in India; less prominent and influential than
other stations, but noted as the door of entrance. Here
began the struggle with Hindooism — intrenched as it
was for ages in the terrible ramparts of caste, " interwoven throughout with false science, false philosophy,
false history, false chronology, false geography," entwined
with every habit, feeling, and action of daily life, among
a people prolific in every form of vice, and demoralized
by long inheritance, till the sense of moral rectitude seemed
extinct. The Hindoos, in some instances, charged the
missionaries with having written the first of Romans on
purpose to describe their case. Hindooism was aided,
too, in its recoil, by the dealings of the English nation,
who, says Sydney Smith, " have exemplified in our public
conduct every crime of which human nature is capable."

In itself, Bombay proved one of the most discouraging
of all the stations of the Board. Sickness and death kep*t*

sweeping away its laborers, and it was years before the
first conversion of a Hindoo.   But one missionary now *
resides at Bombay, and that city is now only one of the
seven stations of the Mahratta mission — numbering
some forty out-stations and thirty-one churches, with a
membership scattered through a hundred and forty villages.   The tremendous strength of Hindooism is well
exhibited in the fact that up to the year 1856, the total
number of conversions in the mission was but two hundred
and eighty-five ; and the sure triumph and accelerating
power of the gospel were equally well expressed in the
fact that for the next six years the conversions were nearly twice as many as in the previous forty, and that never
has there been such depth of interest, and so numerous
accessions from the higher castes, as during the last few
years.   The seed-time has been long and wearisome.   The
full harvest-time is not yet come.   But Hindooism is felt
to be undermined ; and another generation may witness,
if the church is faithful, such revolutions in India as there
is not now faith to believe.   The details of this long struggle, could they be here recounted, would present a record
of faithful unfaltering toil, rather than of striking incidents.   When once the missionaries were admitted, the
strong hand of British power became their protection.
There were many excitements, and there were sore trials
on the part of those who often were called literally to
abandon father and mother for Christ.   But it was a rare
thing when, in 1832, the missionaries were hooted and
pelted with dirt in the streets of Ahmednuggur, and their
preaching assemblies broken up.

The field is intrinsically difficult, and this mission was
the first experiment of the Board.   Experience has led,
within the last few years, to some modifications in

* 1871.

method, from which, in connection with the large preparatory work already accomplished, greater results may reasonably be looked for. Less relative importance is attached to local printing and teaching, and far more to itinerant preaching and personal intercourse. Failure to reach the women was found to be not only a great obstacle to rapid progress, but the cause of many a relapse. The attempt to give an English education indiscriminately in the schools proved to be more than unprofitable, in a missionary point of view, since the knowledge of English often became an inducement to abandon the missionary. Perhaps too little dependence also had been placed on native piety to maintain its own institutions, and organize aggressive movements. These things have begun to receive the most earnest attention. A native pastorate, missionary tours, self-support of the churches, heavier benevolent contributions, and greatly increased labors by women among the women, are omens of a time at hand when the gospel in India shall rest upon home forces and win its own way.

The establishment of the Mahratta mission at Bombay was followed in 1816 by the mission to Ceylon, among a Tamil-speaking people, and in 1834 by the Madura mission, among the kindred Tamil people on the Continent. A glance at these three regions of India at the present time would show at the Mahratta mission, centring at Ahmednugger, some forty-seven stations and outstations, including twenty-one churches with six hundred and twenty-nine communicants. The little band of ten missionaries, with their wives, is re-enforced by eleven native pastors, three preachers, nine catechists, twenty-seven teachers, fourteen Bible women, and twenty-four other helpers. While the church members themselves are scattered through a hundred and forty villages, an organized system of itinerant preaching carried the gospel message, in 1870, to many hundred villages and sixty thousand or seventy thousand hearers. A theological class of six is coming forward, the church members are beginning to rally in earnest to the support of their ministry, Bible women are working their way into the families; and it was a day to be remembered when a native Christian Alliance, with a hundred and fifty representative men, was lately held at Bombay, to impress upon each other the duty of independent labor to propagate the gospel in India. Their discussions were earnest and practical, and filled with " evidences of deeper feeling than was ever seen before in Bombay."

But the struggle of the gospel in this region must still be a mighty conflict. The laborers are few, too few for anything like an aggressive movement. The Mahratta country, of which Bombay is the capital, extends three hundred miles on the coast and four hundred and fifty miles inland, with a population of eleven millions. What are ten missionaries to such a population? They are contending with ignorance so dense that but five persons in a hundred can read at all, and few of them intelligently. And as to the general level of intelligence, Mr. Bissell has well said, " The Hindoo knows nothing that is worth knowing, and what he thinks he knows is a delusion;" " false geography, false astronomy, false history," held with all the tenacity of false religion. They contend with a caste-system so divisive, that not only the touch, but the very shadow, of a Mahar is pollution to a Brahmin; so terribly rigid, that when Vishnupunt, now pastor at Ahmednuggur, became a Christian, his parents performed funeral rites for him. Their son was " dead."

They contend with an idolatry dreadfully benumbing to the mind and the heart; that burnt widows and swung on hooks as long as it was suffered; that still worships the cobra di capello and the crow; that reckons it as great a charity to preserve the life of an animal as of a man; that actually built its poorhouses in Bombay for superannuated cows, cats, and dogs, but never a poorhouse in all India for human beings; that replies to the preacher, " A full stomach is my heaven," and, " You may as well play on a lute to a buffalo; " and that, even when convinced of its lost condition, could come, as did Yesoba, and pour its bag of rupees on the floor, with the words, " Sahib, take this money and give me salvation." They contend, too, with the adverse influence of a corrupt European civilization, and the counter-agency of open European infidelity, which has its organs even in Bombay, and which often fills with Deism the void in the mind of the educated Hindoo.

But with all this they have fought and begun to conquer. Yesoba, with his bag of rupees, found the Saviour, and lived and died in the faith. The Brahmin and the Mahar drink of one cup in the Christian church. Mr. Bruce records with wonder the change he found in the villages of Punchegav in 1870. Twelve years before, the *patil*, or head man, ordered the missionary out of the place with language of awful foulness. The second visit was resisted by the people themselves *en masse*. On a third visit three missionaries could not find a soul to listen. And when at length Harkaba, an honored teacher, became converted, " Beat him," " Kill him," " Bury him," were the fierce utterances of the enraged villagers. They could not fulfil their threats; but they often made old Harkaba flee into the jungle to weep and pray. But now the same *patil* gave the missionary a cordial welcome, and offered to give the little church a piece of land for a chapel; an evening lecture filled the "rest-house" full of people, and a hundred stood outside. This is certainly an unusual change. But there is, no doubt, a steadily increasing number of intelligent natives, who feel as did one, — a wealthy and influential man, — whom Mr. Bissel encountered in a little village on a missionary tour. "Sahib," said he, "your religion is true, and it will prevail in this land. If we do not embrace it, our children will; or if they do not, *their* children will, for it is true and must prevail."

A little group of eleven churches, with five hundred and thirty members, occupy the northern province of Ceylon, an island of two million inhabitants, once swept over by Francis Xavier with forty thousand so-called "converts." Here is the region where Richards, and Meigs, and Poor, and Scudder began their missionary work, and where Spaulding has faithfully toiled for more than half a century. The churches lie scattered among the rural districts and the cultivators of the soil, where one hundred and eighty thousand inhabitants of the Jaffna province are provided with five hundred and fifty heathen temples, holding their annual festivals, more impressive with pomp, and more insnaring with vice, to that sensual people, than can well be conceived. The festivals are Satan's grand gala-days, and the temples around which they gather are Satan's stronghold. It has been mostly a sappers' and miners' work, and not assault and storm. The mission began at Batticotta and Tillipally, in the ruins of two Portuguese churches older than the settlement of America, and at Oodooville, in the residence of an ancient Franciscan friar. In about three years from

their first occupancy began (in 1819) the series of revivals, which, in the early history of this mission, carried it
steadily onward.   They were frequent in the schools.   It
was a delightful time in 1824, when the Spirit of the Lord
came down almost simultaneously on the schools at Tillipally, Oodooville, Batticotta, Manepy, and Pandeteripo.
There was weeping for sins.   There was praying by night
in companies and alone, " the voice of supplication heard
in every quarter," out in the garden at Pandeteripo, each
company or individual " praying as though all were alone,"
and coming in with the weeping inquiry, " What shall
we do to be saved?"   Sixty-nine were thought to have
found the Lord at that precious time.   More than once
did the schools at Batticotta, Oodooville, and Tillipally
experience ·these simultaneous revivals, extending also
to the adult population of the towns.   Every year witnessed admissions to the church, rising in one year (1831)
to sixty-one.

The British government, though admitting the first few
missionaries, had steadily refused, till the year 1833, to
permit any increase of their number.   And yet the little
band had made steady progress.   In a dozen years from
their landing, they were preaching regularly to two thousand hearers on the Sabbath, they were hopefully itinerat-
ing in the villages, and they had forty-five hundred pupils
in their ninety-three free schools, their boarding schools,
and their seminary at Batticotta.   They had gained the
hearty co-operation of the associate justice, and other
distinguished gentlemen of Ceylon, and raised their seminary to so high a repute that where once it was difficult
to procure a pupil, now they selected their entering class
of twenty-nine from two hundred applicants.   In 1833,
the government restriction having been removed, a re-

enforcement of seven missionaries, including a physician and a printer, arrived. Their coming was signalized by the establishment, next year, of a mission (the Madura mission) among the kindred Tamil people on the Continent. Converts were added in Ceylon for the next three years, seventy-nine, fifty-two, forty-nine. And in 1837, with one hundred and eighty-seven free schools, containing seven thousand pupils, a hundred and fifty students in the seminary, and ninety-eight girls in the school at Oodooville, and a rising tide of respect and influence all around, it seemed as though victory was organized.

But that year brought a stunning blow. The failure of the funds from America, in that time of pecuniary trouble, compelled the mission to disband a hundred and seventy schools, to dismiss more than five thousand children, including a part of the pupils in the two seminaries, to stop their building, curtail their printing, and cut down to the very quick. Their Sabbath congregations were nearly broken up, all their activities razeed, their spirits discouraged, and their hearts almost broken. It was a time of woe. The heathen exulted. Native converts were discouraged and led astray. Educated and half-educated youth were snatched away from under the gospel, and often worse than lost to the cause. And though in the following year the home churches were startled into furnishing the funds once more, and the mission kept thanksgiving over the restoration, it may be doubted whether it has ever recovered its lost headway and its firm hold upon the country. The well-grown tree had been pulled up by the roots. May such havoc never be wrought again.

The missionaries experienced another great shock in

1843, when they discovered the old Hindoo leaven breaking out in the Batticotta seminary in such falsehood and gross vices as necessitated the expulsion of sixty-one pupils, including the whole select class, and the dismission of several native teachers. It was one of those fearful pieces of surgery which the constitutional rottenness of heathenism may sometimes require. Outwardly, the wound healed over in a year, and the school was more flourishing than before.

No striking events have occurred within the last few years. Marked revivals, though not unknown, are less frequent than they once were. The novelty, and, per haps, prestige of the gospel have long passed by, and it takes its place by the other religions, to contend for the land by a long-continued struggle. But the mission is organized for work, and its churches are in a transition state toward self-support. Five native pastors, three other native preachers, fourteen catechists, and seventy-eight teachers are re-enforcing the missionaries; while the Batticotta "Training and Theological School," with its twenty students, and the female boarding schools at Oodooville and Oodoopitty, with seventy-six pupils, are raising a further supply, and twenty-six hundred children are gathered in the village schools, which are now aided and partly controlled by the British government. All the villages of the province are now accessible to the gospel, and, from time to time, many of them are visited by the missionaries, or by native preachers, catechists, and colporters, going from house to house, gathering congregations when they can, and making known the truth. Weekly conferences, and mothers' meetings in the churches, a religious paper (The Morning Star), and the "Native Evangelical Society," a Board of Foreign

Missions, with its " annual meetings and reports," and
" special appeals " for an occasional debt, crowned with
success, its chapel-buildings, where the remaining debt
(as at Pungerative last year) is cleared off on dedication
day, — all begin to remind one of the mother country on
a small scale. These things, with the increasing dependence on the native agencies, and the movement for more
effective influence upon the women by their own sex, are
pointing forward to a time when these home agencies
shall take care of themselves. The missionary force is
at present inadequate to the best economy and activity,
and formidable foes are to be encountered. A tide of
educated infidelity also increases the semblance of a civilized land. Thus the first two natives who received the
degree of A. B. at Madras University, on the Continent,
turned against Christianity. At the same time there is
apparently a wide-spread intellectual conviction of its
truth among those who refuse to submit to its claims.
The posture of things is well indicated in the case of two
persons with whom Mr. De Riemer had a recent inter-
view — a young Brahmin and an old Sivite priest whom
he brought with him. The young Brahmin boldly as-
serts the sin and folly of idolatry, and is greatly interested in the gospel, but cannot gain strength to cut
the cord that his wife, family, and rank bind around
him, and come out for Christ. The old Sivite priest (or
gooroo), for sixty years an attendant on one of the largest
temples, lamented not only his waning star, but the growing neglect and disrespect of the people for their gooroos.
And when asked if this were not an omen of the day
when the gospel would supplant the whole religion, he
raised both hands and exclaimed, " Undoubtedly! Most

D

certainly! The time is very near at hand. Only a few days." Would it were true. But the end is not yet.

The Madura mission embraces the "Madura Collectorate," an oblong district of about eighty-eight hundred square miles, containing a population of some two millions, scattered through nearly four thousand villages, and speaking the Tamil language. The city of Madura lies near the centre. In the midst of this population eleven ordained missionaries and a physician, with their wives and other ladies, occupied, in 1870, thirteen stations and a hundred and fifty out-stations. They had clustered round them twenty-eight churches, with fourteen hundred communicants, including eight native pastors, a hundred and twenty-two catechists, and a band of teachers. A newly-formed theological school at Pasumalai, with twenty-two students, is raising a further supply of young ministers, preaching as they study. A regularly organized system of itinerant preaching has in one year reached twelve or thirteen hundred villages and seventy thousand hearers. The church collections, for local and other purposes, have reached, by a steady increase, thirty-two hundred rupees a year. An Evangelical Alliance is aiding the churches toward self-support. Bible women are pleasantly received; and the change in many homes is such that the missionary has ventured to remind his congregations, that once they had "donkeys in their houses, but now friends and companions." Opposition, and even downright persecution, are not wanting. In a village near Madura, recently, a little band of Christians were, by artful accusations, brought eight times before the police, and twice lodged in jail. But "stolid indifference" is the chief obstacle — utter animal life. The signs of promise, however, are not few. The churches

are more effectually reaching the higher castes. Mr.
Washburn reports twenty-five hundred Bibles, or portions of the Bible, *sold* in nine years around the station
of Battalagundu. A Brahmin reported that the income
of the temple at Tirupuvanam had fallen off forty per
cent. in four years. The persecution near Madura oc-
casioned a meeting of the friends and relatives to consider the question of joining the persecuted. And in
parts of the field occasional facts recall the scenes of
early Jewish and of later Christian lands. Mr. Chandler,
in 1870, encountered a representative of Christ's own
hearers in a man of wealth and high caste, who has read
Christian books, and will build a school-house for a Christian school, who says he " believes in the Christian religion, and would embrace it but for certain family ties,
from which he cannot now break away." And Mr. Tracy,
later still, found in Madura just such persons as we find
at home — young men, intelligent, educated, amiable,
denouncing the follies of idolatry, cordially admitting
Bible truths, acknowledging even their own sin, but
strenuously refusing Christ and an atonement, with the
declaration that " repentance was the only atonement
needful."

In view of this state of things, it will not be surprising
if, with God's blessing and a sufficient working force, the
next ten years shall show great changes in this field, for
which the church has great encouragement to pray, and
look, and give. Two significant facts arrest the attention : More than four fifths of these church members have
been gathered during the last half of the time, and they
represent twenty different castes.

In this goodly work have been found engaged some of
the choicest spirits that the church has seen since apos-

tolic times. The names of Hall, and Newell, and Poor,
and Scudder, and Meigs, and Hoisington, and Winslow,
and Ballantine, and many others now with God, are names
of blessed memory and holy fragrance. And where are
the like-minded men to enter in and finish the work? It
was theirs to open the field to the Christian world : who
will follow? The task is well begun. " There will probably be," said an intelligent observer, " a long preparatory work in India, and a rapid development."

Hitherto the enterprise has been carried on amid discouragements, oppositions, private persecutions, and even
poisonings of converts ; but it has steadily gone forward.
And when we see the accelerated motion with which the
gospel is now pushing its way, when we view men of the
higher castes coming in and the whole fearful enginery
of caste giving way, when we see the gathering of the
Christian denominations toward India, and listen to the
confessions of the Hindoo organs and leaders, we sometimes think the harvest may not be far away.

And to-day, over against the despairing cry of Martyn,
and the dogged assertion of Sydney Smith, we will put
the admission of the *Indu Prakash*, the native Bombay
newspaper : " We daily see Hindoos, of every caste,
becoming Christians and devoted ' missionaries of the
cross.' " And so far as figures can show the power of
a movement that runs deeper than all figures, ponder the
following statistics, carefully compiled in 1862. In the
three Presidencies of India there were representatives
of thirty-one missionary societies at work, aided by ninety-
eight ordained native preachers. They were regularly
dispensing the gospel to one thousand one hundred and
ninety congregations, besides hundreds of thousands
of other hearers ; they reckoned a hundred and thirty-

eight thousand registered or nominal Christians, of
whom thirty-one thousand were communicants; they
had ninety thousand children and youth in attendance on
their schools.

These facts are to be viewed as only the foundation,
long laid in silence below the surface, for vastly greater
changes yet to appear. So deep is the hold of the work,
not only on the native converts, but on the foreign residents, that, the churches themselves already (1867) contribute twenty-five thousand dollars a year; while British
residents in India give a hundred thousand dollars annually to the several missionary societies in that country.

And could the witty writer of the *Edinburgh* now visit
the scene, he might incline, in several particulars, to modify
his judgment of 1808 — that the missionaries " would deliberately, piously, and conscientiously expose our whole
Eastern empire to destruction, for the sake of converting
half a dozen Brahmins, who, after stuffing themselves
with rum and rice, and borrowing money from the missionaries, would run away, and cover the gospel and its
professors with every species of ridicule and abuse." He
might be glad, also, to sum up his case a little differently
than thus: " Shortly stated, then, our argument is this:
We see not the slightest prospect of success; we see much
danger in the attempt, and we doubt if the conversion of
the Hindoos would ever be more than nominal." It is a
marvelous specimen of the folly of this world's wisdom,
and a strong showing how God hath chosen the weak
things of this world to confound the mighty.

Never was an enterprise begun and prosecuted with a
deeper sense of helplessness without God, and of whole-
souled trust in his power and his promise. Judson has
well expressed the spirit that animated all his comrades.

When he had been three years at his post, and had found
neither a convert, an inquirer, nor an interested listener,
he could write thus : " If any ask, What prospect of ulti-
mate success is there ? tell them, As much as that there is
an almighty and faithful God. . . . If a ship was lying
in the river, ready to convey me to any part of the world
I should choose, and that, too, with the entire approba-
tion of all my Christian friends, I would prefer dying to
embarking." Two years more witnessed but one inquirer — yet the same song of faith and hope : " I have
no doubt that God is preparing the way for the conversion of Burmah to his Son. This thought fills me with
joy. I know not that I shall live to see a single convert ;
but, notwithstanding, I feel that I would not leave my
present situation to be made a king."

Such was the dauntless courage that led the first Foreign Mission of the American churches ; such the first
handful of Christian soldiers that deliberately sat down
to the siege of all India — to whom God gave the victory.
How sublime that faith ! How glorious the reward !
" He that goeth forth and weepeth, bearing precious
seed, shall doubtless come again with rejoicing, bringing his sheaves with him." Let Christians and churches
ponder well the struggle of the gospel for a foothold in
India, and never again entertain one doubt of the sacred
promise, " Lo ! I am with you alway, even unto the end
of the world."

March, 1876.

The foregoing sketch was prepared in 1871, and the
statistics given are for that year, — of course not correct
as matters stand now. But in bringing out a new edition,
it is thought best to use the stereotype plates much as they

were left four years ago, simply appending here a few paragraphs, as to the present condition of the missions.

New laborers have gone to each of the fields. The reinforcements to the Mahratta mission have been, Miss Sarah F. Norris, M. D., in 1873; Rev. Robert A. Hume and wife, and Miss Martha A. Anderson in 1874; Wm. O. Ballantine M. D. and wife, Rev. Edward S. Hume and wife, and Rev. Lorin S. Gates and wife, in 1875. Miss Elizabeth Sisson joined the Madura mission in 1872; Rev. Messrs. Wm. S. Howland and John S. Chandler, with their wives, in 1873; and Rev. M. R. Peck and wife in 1875. Rev. Samuel W. Howland and wife, and Miss Susan R. Howland went to Ceylon in 1873. It is well worthy of notice that of these twenty persons eleven are children of parents who are, or have been, connected with these missions, namely, the three Howlands, the two Humes and both their wives (formerly Miss Burgess and Miss Chandler), Dr. Ballantine (three of whose sisters had before returned to India as the wives of missionaries), Mr. Chandler and his wife (formerly Miss Minor), and Mrs. Gates, formerly Miss Hazen. Nine of the laborers now connected with the Mahratta mission were born in that field. Educated in America, they have returned to carry on the evangelizing work so well begun by their parents.

No special change has taken place in the character or conditions of the missionary work unless a decided increase of effort among women may be regarded as such a change. In these, as in nearly all foreign fields, "woman's work for woman" has greatly increased of late. In the Mahratta field, the missionary ladies, as a native pastor testifies, "without neglecting household duties, somehow make time for this work," and "it is owing to their efforts that

so many women are brought into the church." In the
Madura field Miss Sisson, and in Ceylon Misses Hillis and
Howland are specially engaged in this department, other
ladies of the missions, and native " Bible women," also
doing much in the same work, which seems to be indeed,
as Miss Sisson reports, " one of much promise ; although
it is but recently that the thick veil of prejudice, which
hides these poor heathen women from our missionary
ladies, has been lifted at all, and the work is still in its infancy."

All the missions are striving to bring forward a better
educated native agency, by means of boarding schools for
girls, and seminaries, and theological and training schools,
or classes for young men. The Jaffna College (not designed to be a mission institution though one in which
the mission feels a deep interest) has been started in
Ceylon with, as yet, quite insufficient funds, but with much
of promise if needed funds to complete a very moderate
endowment can be secured. There are now, in the three
missions, 39 native pastors, while about 120 other natives
are engaged as preachers and catechists in evangelizing
work.

Additions to the churches by profession, during the last
four calendar years reported, have been as follows, and
show gratifying progress : —

	1872	1873	1874	1875
Mahratta Mission	37	76	116	126
Madura Mission	117	127	123	182
Ceylon Mission	41	27	44	80
Totals	195	230	283	388

The following table presents other

STATISTICS OF THE MISSION IN 1875.

	Stations.	Out-stations.	Ordained Missionaries.	Other males from the U. S.	Females.	Native Pastors.	Preachers and Catechists.	Other native helpers.	Churches.	Members.	Male pupils in Seminaries.	Female pupils in Seminaries.	Pupils in Com. Schools.
Mahratta Mission . .	6	56	11	1	15	15	5	92	23	868		100	965
Madura Mission . .	11	148	12	1	16	17	103	150	32	1880	153	114	2,862
Ceylon Mission . .	7	12	5	1	10	7	14	30	12	679	34	92	5,926*
Total	23	216	28	3	41	39	122	272	67	3,427	187	306	9,753

It may be well to present here a few statements in regard to the general missionary work in India — its progress and its prospects, — by quoting briefly from an article published in the London " Quarterly Review " for April, 1875, and also from a more recent article in the " Foreign Missionary," of the Presbyterian Board, for January, 1876. The " Quarterly " states : —

" A considerable change in the feelings with which Indian missions are regarded has recently taken place. The emphatic testimony of the Indian Government in their favor has already produced a marked effect on the public mind, an instance of which is apparent even in an article on ' Christian Missions ' in a recent number of the ' Westminster Review,' in which the writer, whilst disparaging missions in general, goes so far as to admit that the results of the Indian missions ' constitute the most brilliant page in the whole history of our missionary enterprise.'

" The number of converts in connection with the various Protestant missions in India, as ascertained by the statistical returns to which we have referred, is much greater

* The common schools connected with this mission are now under the care of a Board of Education, and are not strictly mission schools.

than it was expected to be. When the results of this religious census were made known, it is hard to say whether the friends of missions or their enemies were most surprised. The total number of native Protestant Christians in 1871 was found to be 318,363; of whom 78,494 were communicants; the number of native ordained ministers was 381; and the amount of money contributed by native Christians alone, for religious and charitable purposes, was £15,912. What is still more remarkable is the rapidity and steadfastness of the ratio of increase. During the ten years previous to 1861 the rate of increase was 53 per cent. During the ten years previous to 1871, the rate of increase rose to 61 per cent. During this last period of ten years, the increase in the number of converts amounted to no fewer than 85,430 souls in India proper alone."

The "Foreign Missionary" says, January, 1876: "To-day the missionary work is carried on in India and Ceylon by thirty-five missionary societies, besides local agencies. In the different Presidencies are 500 ordained missionaries, occupying more than 400 stations and over 2,000 sub-stations, the latter chiefly manned by native laborers." After giving various statistics of the work, it adds: —

"These results of missionary labor are great and wonderful, but other changes, through the pressure of Christian sentiment and the power of truth, have taken place. In 1825 the Government abetted idolatry, and sought no alliance with Christianity. It husbanded the endowments of temples and mosques; it supplied funds from its treasury for repairing temples and roads to sacred places; it taxed pilgrims, and endowed schools for the teaching of error and superstition. Then infanticide abounded; Suttees flourished; bloody rites were practiced. Then no Christian convert could obtain his rights in regard to property. These and kindred evils existed. Now all is changed. Government protects and aids missionary operations; it has cut itself loose from all connection with idolatry; infanticide is declared a criminal act; Suttee is prohibited; and cruel rites have been forbidden. The Koran and the Ganges water are banished from the courts of justice. Converts are protected in their rights, and the legal validity of widows re-marrying is proclaimed. Hindooism is losing its hold upon the many, and the idea is growing that it must disappear under the power of Christianity. There is an enlarging circle that has broken with Brahminism, though not yet yielding openly to the religion of Jesus. Signs of improvement — material, social, intellectual, and moral — fill the land. The natives are awakening from the sleep of ages; the desire for sound knowledge is growing. Caste is relaxing. Stereotyped customs, that have been more powerful than law, are disappearing. A knowledge of the Bible is speading, its precepts are becoming more influential, and the truth is working wonders among the aborigines, who never yielded to Hindoo or Mohammedan influence, but are now accepting joyfully the doctrines of the Cross.

" Christianity has obtained a firm footing. Its ambassadors are alive to the importance of its dissemination, and are increasing in numbers and skill. Native churches have been planted all over the land, and these are becoming more potential for good."

MISSIONARIES, 1876.	Went Out.	Station.
MAHRATTA MISSION.		
Rev. Samuel B. Fairbank	1846	Ahmednuggur.
Mrs. Mary B. Fairbank	1856	
Rev. Allen Hazen, D. D.	1846	Bombay.
Mrs. Martha R. Hazen	1846	
Rev. Lemuel Bissell, D. D.	1851	Ahmednuggur.
Mrs. Mary E. Bissell	1851	
Rev. Charles Harding	1856	Sholapoor.
Mrs. Elizabeth D. Harding . . .	1869	
Rev. Henry J. Bruce	1862	Satara.
Mrs. Hepzibeth P. Bruce	1862	
Rev. W. H. Atkinson	1867	Sholapoor.
Mrs. Calista Atkinson	1867	
Rev. S. R. Wells	1869	Bhuing.
Mrs. Mary L. Wells	1869	
Rev. Charles W. Park	1870	Bombay.
Mrs. Anna M. Park	1870	
Rev. Richard Winsor	1870	Satara.
Mrs. Mary C. Winsor	1870	
Miss Harriet S. Ashley	1871	Bombay.
Miss Sarah F. Norris, M. D. . . .	1873	Bombay.
Rev. Robert A. Hume	1874	Ahmednuggur.
Mrs. Abbie S. Hume	1874	
Miss Martha A. Anderson	1874	Ahmednuggur.
William O. Ballantine, M. D. . . .	1875	Rahoori.
Mrs. Alice C. Ballantine	1875	
Rev. Edward S. Hume	1875	Ahmednuggur.
Mrs. Charlotte E. Hume	1875	
Rev. Lorin S. Gates	1875	Sholapoor.
Mrs. Frances A. Gates	1875	
MADURA MISSION.		
Rev. William Tracy, D. D.	1836	Tirupuvanam.
Mrs. Emily F. Tracy		
Mrs. Martha S. Taylor	1844	Mandapasalai.
Rev. John Rendall	1845	Battalagundu.
Rev. James Herrick	1845	Tirumangalam.
Mrs. Elizabeth H. Herrick	1845	
Rev. John E. Chandler	1845	Madura.
Mrs. Charlotte H. Chandler . . .	1845	
Rev. Thomas S. Burnell	1848	Melûr.
Mrs. Martha Burnell	1848	
Rev. Joseph T. Noyes	1848	Periakulam.
Mrs. Elizabeth A. Noyes	1848	
Rev. W. B. Capron	1856	Mana Madura.
Mrs. Sarah B. Capron	1856	

MISSIONARIES, 1876.	Went Out.	Station
Rev. Edward Chester	1858	Dindigul.
Mrs. Sophia Chester	1858	
Rev. George T. Washburn	1860	Pasumalai.
Mrs. Eliza E. Washburn	1860	
Miss Martha S. Taylor	1867	Mandapasalai.
Miss Mary E. Rendall	1870	Battalagundu.
Miss Elizabeth Sisson	1872	Madura.
Rev. William S. Howland	1873	Mandapasalai.
Mrs. Mary L. Howland	1873	
Rev. John S. Chandler	1873	Madura.
Mrs. Jennie E. Chandler	1873	
Rev. Marshall R. Peck	1875	
Mrs. Helen N. Peck	1875	
CEYLON MISSION.		
Miss Eliza Agnew	1839	Ooodooville.
Rev. William W. Howland	1845	Tillipally.
Mrs. Susan R. Howland	1845	
Rev. Eurotas P. Hastings	1846	Batticotta.
Mrs. Anna Hastings	1846	
Samuel F. Green, M. D.	1847	Manepy.
Mrs. Margaret W. Green	1862	
Miss Harriet E. Townshend	1867	Oodoopitty.
Rev. William E. De Riemer . . .	1868	Chavagacherry
Mrs. Emily F. De Riemer	1868	
Miss Hester A. Hillis	1870	Manepy.
Rev. Thomas S. Smith	1871	Oodoopitty.
Mrs. Emily M. Smith	1871	
Rev. Samuel W. Howland	1873	Oodooville.
Mrs. Mary E. K. Howland . . .	1873	
Miss Susan R. Howland	1873	Manepy.

HISTORICAL SKETCH

OF THE

MISSIONS OF THE AMERICAN BOARD

AMONG THE

NORTH AMERICAN INDIANS.

BY

REV. S. C. BARTLETT, D. D.

BOSTON:
PUBLISHED BY THE BOARD,
1 SOMERSET STREET.
1876.

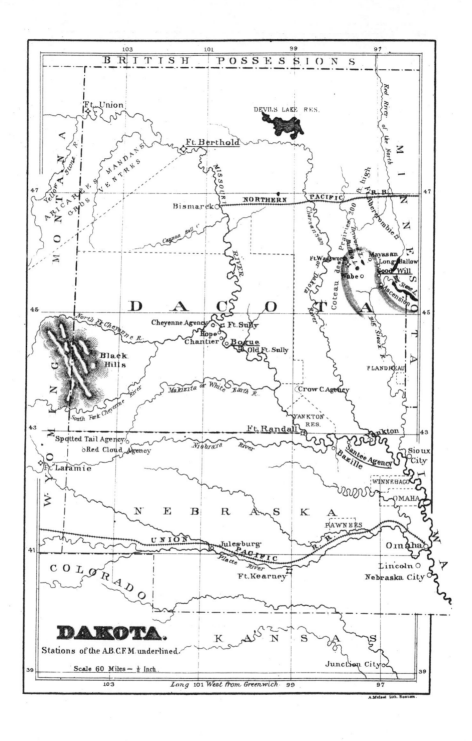

A. Meisel. Lith. Boston.

BARTLETT'S SKETCHES

MISSIONS AMONG THE NORTH AMERICAN INDIANS.

IT has been often said, You can not tame an Indian. The statement betrays a singular ignorance of facts. No more docile pagans have been found than some of the North American tribes. Seldom have earlier fruits been reaped than in the Indian missions; seldom have brighter promises of a glorious harvest been blasted by adverse events and wicked interferences.

It has been so from the first. Within a year of the landing at Plymouth, Elder Cushman informed his friends in England of the "tractable disposition" of the Indian youth. As early as 1643, John Eliot had been through "varieties of intercourse with them, day and night, summer and winter, by land and by sea," and had had "many solemn discourses with all sorts of nations of them, from one end of the country to another."

Probably by this time commenced the long-continued and successful labors of Bourne and Tupper at Marshpee. And in 1646 began, in good earnest, the preaching of Mayhew on Martha's Vineyard, and of Eliot around Newton.

Eliot's work has become historical. The index and monument of his achievements and his prospects is found in that famous Indian Bible — the first, and long the only, Bible printed in America. It has scarcely one

1

living reader now ; yet thirty-five hundred copies of it once issued from the Cambridge press. Eliot had, in 1674, a circuit of fourteen villages, and eleven hundred praying Indians. Next year came the terrible blight of " Philip's War," and cut down his congregations to four. They never recovered from the shock. In fact, only their Christian connections saved the whole of them from extinction at the time. The suspicions, jealousies, irritations, and revenges then aroused never ceased. Then began the long catalogue of organized Indian miseries. The General Court collected the remnant, and *removed* them to the islands in the bay, where they suffered " incredible hardships ; " and the five hundred removed had, in 1698, shrunk to two hundred and five Indians in all what was then Massachusetts proper. Removal! The old, old story, ever new ; the fatal rock of all their prospects.

In the next century, various efforts were equally hopeful, and equally frustrated. The relics of the Mohegans, at Stockbridge, were gathered by John Sergeant into a thriving town, with twenty houses, built in English style, and a church of forty communicants. The Revolutionary War made, in various modes, sad havoc among them ; and after the war, they *removed*, first to Central New York, then to Indiana, then to Green Bay, then to Lake Winnebago. A relic of them remained in New York, and were transferred, in 1827, with the relics of other tribes, to the care of the American Board. But in all their removals, averaging one for every twenty or twenty-five years, the tribe never lost its civilization. An early and most hopeful mission of the Moravians to the Indians of New York was thrice broken up by fire and sword, and three or four times broken down by removals. David Brainerd's mission in New Jersey, and the opening efforts of Eleazer Wheelock's Indian school and college, with its various Indian missionaries, seem to have been almost fatally interrupted by the struggles, absorptions, and complications of the Revolutionary War.

A generation passed away. Within three years and a half of the time when Hall and his associates sailed for India, the American Board was adopting measures (1815) for carrying the gospel to the Indians. One hundred thousand of them were then supposed to reside east of the Mississippi, of whom about seventy thousand were comprised in the four southern tribes — Creeks, Chickasaws, Choctaws, and Cherokees. The Prudential Committee, whose previous purposes had " from time to time been frustrated," now brought the matter in earnest before the Board and the Christian public. They appealed to the success with which Rev. Gideon Blackburn, of the Presbyterian Church, had already labored among the Cherokees, in five years enabling four or five hundred youth to read the English Bible, and receiving several individuals as " hopeful and exemplary Christians." Before another annual meeting, the first Indian missionary of the American Board, Cyrus Kingsbury, fresh from Andover Seminary, had visited the Cherokees. He passed through Washington, on the way, where a Cherokee chief expressed his deep interest in the effort. He said that his nation had long wished for schools, and had even " thought of devoting a part of their annuity to the object." President Madison also ordered the Secretary of War to say that the Agent for Indian Affairs would erect a house for the school, and one for the teacher, to be followed by others, as occasion

might require, and success might justify.   The agent
would also be instructed to make the munificent provision
of " two plows, six hoes, and as many axes, for the purpose of introducing the art of cultivation among the pupils," and when female pupils should be received, and a
female teacher engaged, " a loom, half a dozen spinning-
wheels, and as many pair of cards."   All these, however, " will remain public property, to be employed for
the benefit of the nation " — a nation of many thousand
souls.   The government would gladly have done more,
but its means were " limited."

Mr. Kingsbury went on his way rejoicing.   In October he had a grand talk with the assembled chiefs of the
Cherokees and the Creeks, at the close of which a
principal chief took him by the hand, and sententiously
informed him: " We have listened to what you have
said, and have understood it.   We are glad to see you.
We wish to have the schools established, and hope they
will be of great benefit to the nation."   Another chief
was appointed to assist in selecting a site, and they fixed
upon Chickamauga, ten miles from the place forty-seven
years later made famous by the repulse of the Union
army, on the banks of the creek which some rebel
termed the River of Death, and seven miles, also, from
the brow of that Lookout Mountain, where, in " the bat-
tle of the clouds," the Confederacy received a stunning
blow.   The missionaries called it Brainerd.   A neighboring height still bears the name of " Mission Ridge."

Mr. Kingsbury, followed at once by Messrs. Hall and
Williams, with their wives, and soon after by others,
immediately began the enterprise.   It was a compound
of mission, boarding-school, and agricultural college.
The beginning, as well as the continuance of it, entailed

immense care and labor upon the missionaries. The government contractor, like many of his successors, failed to build the houses agreed upon, and the missionaries soon found themselves engaged in making twenty thousand bricks, burning lime, digging cellars and a well, besides the by-play of bringing their meal forty miles, and planting " twenty or thirty acres of corn, some cotton, flax, and potatoes," to say nothing of a school of twenty-six young Cherokees, a Sunday school of thirty blacks, and preaching on the Sabbath. In eighteen months the Treasurer of the Board visited the mission, and was delighted. He found the Indian boys alike willing to work, docile to learn, and orderly and gentle in their behavior. They could plant an acre of corn before breakfast; fifteen of them could read in the Bible, and eleven in easy lessons; and eighteen could write. Their deportment at prayers, at table, at school, would have been creditable to white children. Five natives were already in the little church, followed the same year by two others. The religious experiences of some of these Indian converts were most striking and refreshing. One day (May 27, 1819) President Monroe, accompanied by General Gaines, suddenly made his appearance, unannounced till he stood at the door. He expressed himself so well pleased with all he saw, that, on the spot, he ordered a much better building for the girls' school, at the public expense.

No wonder the friends of missions took courage. Christian farmers and mechanics offered their aid. Meanwhile the committee determined to push on to the Chickasaws and Choctaws, who ardently desired them to do so. Accordingly, in 1818, Mr. Kingsbury selected a site among the Choctaws, on the Yazoo, four hundred

miles south-west of Brainerd, and called it Eliot. He
found intemperance already there to an alarming extent,
and the vicious whites who introduced and fostered it.
Here again the first work was chiefly of secular arrangement. A dense forest covered the ground, although the
works of the ancient mound-builders, here and there,
indicated a former population in the wilderness. Amid
the sickness of acclimation, and innumerable difficulties
and hardships, in eight months they had erected some
ten log buildings for various uses, the lumber all hewed
and sawed by hand; cleared and inclosed thirty-five
acres of land; set out fruit trees; besides cutting roads,
building small bridges, and even making tools and furniture. So eager were the Choctaws for instruction that
eight children were brought a hundred and sixty miles
before the missionaries were ready, and the school was
prematurely opened in April (1819), under this con-
straint. When opened, more scholars applied than could
be received. The Choctaw king promised two hundred
dollars annually from the nation's annuity; and at a
council, in August, a subscription was made of seven
hundred dollars, eighty-five cows and calves, and five
hundred dollars a year from the annuity. In one year
from that date, the nation, acting in three several districts, voted to devote to the schools their entire annuity
of six thousand dollars from the sale of lands to the
United States. The official letters of the nation, an-
nouncing this fact, express the earnest hope of " taking
their place among the enlightened nations of the land ; "
they overflow with gratitude to their " good, white brothers," and they add that " more than one thousand children in our nation are waiting and looking up to our
white brothers for instruction."

Among the Choctaws, the missionaries, however, were doomed to incessant annoyances and hindrances, chiefly from the slanderous reports and vile influences of renegade whites, who had fled from the restraints of civilized life, and were the sworn enemies of the missionaries. For these, and perhaps other reasons, among the Choctaws, conversions lingered. But with the Cherokees, everything moved steadily forward. It is believed that from the first there was no year without conversions. "Wicked Jack" becomes a new man, and chooses the significant name of John Crawfish. Six members of one family connection (the Sanders family), men and women grown, are received into the church at one time, dedicating their households, too; and "there is not a dry eye in the house." Old John Sanders says "he can sit all night to hear the word of God;" Alexander, though tempted, "would not touch a drop of whisky for five hundred dollars;" and the brothers all became lay-missionaries at once. Catharine Brown, after "eminently adorning the doctrine of God" for six years, dies in blessed peace. David Sanders's little girl, fatally burned, passes away in prayer. John Arch, the interpreter, who had come a hundred and fifty miles to school, offering his gun for clothing, so "wild and forbidding" in appearance that the missionaries shrunk from receiving him till he almost forced himself in — he, too, after five years of Christian life, leaves "evidence of love to God and man much beyond what is common in the best organized Christian communities." The chief, Rising Sun, comes to secure a school and a pious blacksmith for his home, and is determined to "obey the Bible." The missionary Butrick, in a tour of two thousand miles, addresses a hundred and fifty meetings, ranging in size from fifty to two hundred persons, and is everywhere received with attention, and often with gratitude. Men came twenty miles to Willstown, and two men twenty-five miles to Carmel, for religious instruction. At the latter station, on the 21st of March, 1824, eighteen persons were received to the church, from " the gray-headed sinner of seventy " to " the youth of eighteen." Mr. Butrick preached, by invitation, the previous autumn, before the National Council. The Council observed the Sabbath during its session, and prohibited all trade or business on that day. Sabbath observance began, indeed, to extend to many villages. In one instance, a man came nineteen miles to inquire when the next Sabbath would arrive, because he and his neighbors were intending afterward to keep it as well as they could. All was hopeful. Arrangements were made for a network of mission schools. In 1822 the king's interpreter came to smoke with the missionaries the silver-hooped " pipe of peace," its bowl the head of a tomahawk, and its stem the handle ; and Path-Killer, the king, and his chiefs, in National Council assembled, expressed the warmest thanks, and came, one by one, from their seats, to take Mr. Hoyt, the missionary, by the hand. The old king visited the schools, in company with a principal chief. The tears flowed incessantly down his dusky cheeks while the children sang ; and both of them most affectionately addressed the school, — the king a second time, — and closed by taking all the scholars by the hand. The nation soon established regular courts of justice, converted its council into a legislative body, and in 1827 appointed a committee to draft a constitution.

Such was the early movement among the Cherokees,

when a singular Providence came to its aid just at this
point. One George Guess (or Sequoyah), a half-breed
Cherokee, about fifty years old, invented the remarkable
Cherokee alphabet. He could neither write nor speak
English, but simply knew that a mark could be made the
sign of a sound. He set himself to work to gather up all
the *syllables* of the Cherokee tongue, which proved to be
eighty-six. He used English letters, and various modifications of them, with some characters of his own. The
whole was so simple that in " three days " a bright
learner could commence letter-writing. When the fact
first came to the notice of the Prudential Committee, in
1825, the Cherokees in Wills Valley had for two years
been corresponding with their countrymen beyond the
Mississippi. In three or four years, half the nation
could read ; and in the solitudes of the forest, one might
often see the trees inscribed with Cherokee. Within a
year of the translation of the four Gospels into their language, the National Council were appropriating money
(1826) for a printing press and types, and a Boston firm
were soon engaged in cutting punches. Guess, it is said,
never became a Christian, and lamented his invention
when he saw it used for circulating the New Testament.
But he could no more recall his alphabet than Erasmus
his Greek Testament, when it had been launched upon
the world.

In 1826, besides the missions to the Cherokees of
Georgia, then numbering seven stations, and that to the
Choctaws of Mississippi, with ten stations, and one to
the Cherokees of Arkansas, two hundred miles beyond
the Mississippi, the Board received several other Indian
missions from the United Foreign Missionary Society,
as follows : Among the Osages of the Neosho, or Grand

River ; the Osages of Missouri ; mixed tribes at Mackinaw ; the Ottawas at Maumee ; the Senecas at Alleghany, Cattaraugus, and Seneca, as also the Tuscaroras in New York. The Osages were a powerful tribe of several thousand. The New York Indians numbered not more than twenty-five hundred souls.

This year, also, the Board took under its charge the little remnant of the Stockbridge tribe, at Green Bay, whose ancestors had enjoyed the ministrations of John Sergeant, President Edwards, and Dr. West, in Massachusetts. Through all their removals, for a hundred years, they had kept alive a school, and probably had exemplary professors of religion among them. Their church had been revived in 1818, and thirty-three members were added to it in 1827 and 1828. They had their choir of singers, and conducted public worship with Bible and hymn-book in hand ; and their whole settlement, of two hundred and fifty souls, bore an aspect of comfort and civilization.

In 1827 the mission to the Chickasaws, which had been begun seven years previous by the Synod of Georgia and South Carolina, was received by the Board.

And now a glance at these missions, about the close of the year 1830, would have shown a singular state of promise all along the line. It seemed as though all things were now ready for one wide ingathering into complete civilization, and into the kingdom of God. Everywhere were centres of light. The traveler would have found half the Cherokees in Georgia able to read, and leavened with eight churches ; while the arts and methods of civilized life were rapidly spreading. There were schools, courts, a legislature, and stringent laws against intemperance and the sale of strong drinks. The

Choctaws, also, had at last been visited by a revival, and during the year, two hundred and fifty persons were received to church fellowship. There was a church among the Chickasaws, and another among the Cherokees of Arkansas. The haughty Chickasaws, in not a few instances, traveled ten miles to an evening meeting, returning by torchlight, in foot-paths full of mud and water; and Mr. Holmes, a teacher, had written, in 1828, "I have never seen a people so hungry for the bread of life." Numerous conversions had just taken place among the Osages, and a few at Mackinaw. About one fifth of the few Stockbridges, at Green Bay, were church members. The Ottawas at Maumee, and the Indians at Tuscarora, Cattaraugus, and Seneca each had their church, their temperance society, and their benevolent organizations. At this time, *three fourths of all the church members in the missions of the American Board were among the Indians; and it was an ascertained fact, that for twenty years the numbers of the Cherokee, Creek, and Choctaw tribes had been steadily increasing.*

But the great southern mission lay upon a volcano, and the next year it burst forth. One blushes to write the truth of history. Greedy white men had their eye upon the fine lands guaranteed forever to the Indian tribes. As early as 1819, an attempt was made by the United States to remove the Cherokees from their reservation. A deputation to Washington, headed by the noble chief, Charles R. Hicks, had baffled the scheme. They had even then pleaded their new hopes of civilization, and the disastrous effects of removal, as the great objection; and when by treaty their remaining lands were secured to them in perpetuity, amid the abounding joy and gratitude of the nation, a hundred thousand acres of the ceded lands were also appropriated as a perpetual school-fund. " This marks, indeed," said the Prudential Committee, " a new and auspicious era."

But alas! the camel's head was already in the cabin window. Once and again, near the beginning of the century, had the tribe been pacified by money payments for lands already occupied by white " squatters." Again, in 1805, under the specious plea that their growing civilization required less territory, another sale had been secured. And now, at the time of which we write, " the irritating proximity of the Indians and white men " — a euphemism for the perpetual intrusion of reckless, lawless whites upon the Indian Territory — suggested the wolf's method of " inducing " all the Indian tribes to remove beyond the Mississippi. A great body of Cherokees were " persuaded " to go in 1819. The Choctaws had ceded a large tract in 1816, and were awaiting further suasion. The tribe of the Chickasaws, whose motto, " Here we rest," still remains embodied in the name *Alabama*, had already made three cessions ; and about the year 1818, the northern tribes also were bought up. The scheme slumbered for a time at the South. But in 1828, the United States Government, pressed by evil agencies behind, began its work. A deputation of the Arkansas Cherokees at Washington, though not authorized, but forbidden by the standing law of the nation, to alienate any portion of their land, consented to a new removal, and the pressure began to be applied to the Cherokees of Georgia, and to the Choctaws, Creeks, and Chickasaws. All four of these tribes were " greatly agitated and distressed " at the prospect of a compulsory removal from lands guaranteed to them by treaty after treaty with the United States. For

several years, it became the one absorbing and distract-
ing theme of the Cherokees. It threw the Choctaws at
once into great trouble, despondency, and violent dissen-
sions, in which the missionaries stood between two fires :
the pagan portion of the nation falsely charging them
with favoring the removal, and the United States authorities regarding and treating them with suspicion and
severity. One is ashamed to write that in September,
1829, United States Commissioners assembled the Choctaws in council, and proposed terms of removal; that a
committee of sixty Choctaws, representing the three districts of the nation, reported almost unanimously against
it, and the whole body of Choctaws approved the report,
and a large proportion of them went home ; that, on the
next day, the Commissioners assembled the remainder,
and by threats of withdrawing the agent, making them
pay the expenses of the treaty, leaving them to the
mercy of state laws, and by bribery of certain chiefs and
their relatives, forced the treaty through, to the "general
indignation" of the great majority of the warriors and
captains ; and that, meanwhile, the presence of the missionaries at the treaty-ground was forbidden by the
United States Commissioners in writing, although the
presence of all other persons was allowed. But these
are dark facts of history. The Cherokees resisted longer.
They felt, like the Choctaws, that it was only the beginning of the end ; and the few that consented earlier did
it in the firm conviction that all would be compelled to
go, and that the last would be the worst off. But the
vise did not finally hold the victim till the year 1836.
In the July previous, the United States sent as Commissioner, to persuade the Cherokees, the Rev. J. F. Schermerhorn. But in vain. In October, another attempt;
R

again in vain.   The Cherokee delegates then departed to
Washington to confer directly with the Secretary of War.
In their absence, within a month, this gospel messenger
called another council of a fraction and faction of the
tribe, got up another delegation and another treaty, which
was soon ratified by the President and Senate; although
the chief, John Ross, and fifteen thousand of the nation
— a vast majority — protested against the treaty in every
stage of its progress, as unsatisfactory, contrary to the
will of the nation, and made with persons wholly un-
authorized.   The treaty was concluded, it is alleged,
with three chiefs and about six hundred men, women, and
children.*   The chiefs were afterward put to death by
the nation for their treachery, though against the efforts
of John Ross.   But the Rev. J. F. Schermerhorn's treaty
stood; and General Winfield Scott, and two thousand
troops, were afterward detailed to execute its provisions.

But the State of Georgia did not wait for the treaty.
Three years before it divided up the whole Cherokee
country into sections of one hundred and forty acres each,
sold them by lottery to its citizens, and extended its laws
and courts over the territory.   Men with white skins
and black hearts rushed in.   They carried gambling, intemperance, lewdness, and outrage among a people broken
and despondent.   The Cherokee laws against intemperance and liquor-selling were overborne by the laws of
Georgia, as were those of the Choctaws by the laws of
Mississippi.   All was demoralization.   There was even
a reaction against the missions, and a direct loss of influence.   The missionaries were viewed as citizens of the
nation that oppressed them, and as representing its re-

---

* New Am. Cyc.   But Rev. W. Willey writes, "Sixty *men*
and *no* chiefs."

ligion ; and, though the missionaries were actually driven out of Georgia into Arkansas, they were suspected as "treaty men."

A singular experience was that of the two missionaries Butler and Worcester, in 1831. In January they and their companions received notification of a law of Georgia, recently enacted, requiring all white men residing on the Cherokee lands to take the oath of allegiance to the State of Georgia, and get a license from the Governor, under penalty, if found there after the 1st of March, of penitentiary imprisonment at hard labor not less than four years. Well knowing this to be in open conflict with their rights under the constitution, laws, and treaties of the general government, they remained at their post. On the 12th of March appeared a detachment of the "Georgia Guard," headed by a colonel. Three of the missionaries were arrested, and taken to the headquarters of the guard. On being brought, by writ of *habeas corpus*, before a County court, the Judge released them on the ground that, as missionaries patronized by the general government, they were in some sense its agents, and not within the range of the law. Forthwith a correspondence ensued between the Governor of Georgia and the President, in which the latter declared that he did not consider them in any sense agents of the government; and the Postmaster-General, to clear the track, made haste to remove Mr. Worcester from the office of postmaster. The Governor now sent warning letters, and the agent of Georgia gave them two days to leave. Messrs. Worcester and Butler frankly, but respectfully, declined. And now appeared once more the Georgia Guard and a Georgia colonel. Messrs. Butler and Worcester were arrested, with a Methodist missionary

(Mr. Trott), and a Cherokee named Proctor. The latter was for two nights chained by the neck to the wall of the house, and by the ankle to Mr. Trott, and marched two days chained by the neck to a wagon ; and Dr. Butler was marched also with a chain about his neck, and part of the time in pitch darkness, with the chain fastened to the neck of a horse. Two Methodist clergymen meeting them, and expressing some sympathy and indignation, the gallant Colonel Nelson cut a stick and gave one a severe blow on the head, and his subordinate, Brooks, dismounted the other, and drove him along the road, compelling him with the bayonet to keep the centre of the road, through mud and mire, pouring out upon the company the vilest obscenities and oaths, and taunting them, " Fear not, little flock." After eleven days' confinement in a filthy log prison, aggravated by every practicable discomfort, a Georgia court (Clayton, J.) sentenced Messrs. Worcester and Butler to four years hard labor in the penitentiary. A memorial was addressed to the President of the United States. But President Andrew Jackson replied by Lewis Cass, the Secretary of War, that he had satisfied himself that the laws of Georgia rendered the acts of Congress " inoperative," and he had no power to interfere. The case was carried to the Supreme Court of the United States, Judge Marshall presiding ; and the action of the Georgia court was reversed and annulled, and the discharge of the prisoners ordered. The court of Georgia refused to obey, and Governor Lumpkin refused to interpose his executive authority to release the prisoners. When, therefore, a generation later, the Union camp-fires blazed on Mission Ridge, as Bragg, and Hardee, and Longstreet fled, defeated and broken, and when Sherman swept all Georgia from Chattanooga

to Savannah, and the Georgia Governor, as he fled, vainly
released a hundred penitentiary criminals to fight for
their native state, it was difficult for some now living
not to remember the days of Nelson, and Clayton, and
Lumpkin.

For fifteen months and more Messrs. Butler and
Worcester lay in the penitentiary. A memorial to the
Chief Executive of the nation, requesting the enforcement
of the decree for their liberation, was prepared; but
they were dissuaded from presenting it, the more easily,
whether wisely or not, because it was well understood
that the President of the United States would not enforce
that mandate of the Supreme Court of the nation. "Old
Hickory" was now a willow wand. They gave notice,
however, of a new motion in court. And now appeared
on the scene two Georgia congressmen, rejoicing in the
allegorical names of Schley and Coffee, to reconcile them
to their bitter cup. These gentlemen, and other personal
friends of the Governor, promised them that they should
be released if the motion were not made. The missionaries conferred with the Prudential Committee. In view
of the facts that their rights had been *judicially* asserted,
that the law itself was now repealed, that their own
speedy liberation was guaranteed, that no executive enforcement of the national judiciary mandate could be
counted on, that it was too late thus to benefit the Cherokee nation, and especially that this might be a case in
which it was for Christians rather to suffer than to appeal
to force, they withdrew the notice of a motion in court,
and were liberated by proclamation of the Governor.

Georgia could well afford to repeal its law and liberate
its prisoners. It had triumphed over the national court,
and handcuffed the national executive. It had mean-

while put in operation such influences as intimidated and compelled the Cherokees to remove. Within eighteen months of the liberation of the missionaries, the white " squatters" on the Cherokee lands were more numerous than the Indians. And yet, under all the pressure of threats, and bribes, and interruption, and corruption, and outrages, so resolute was the opposition of the nation, that, as we have seen, no treaty of cession could by any fair means be secured. Even when Rev. J. F. Scher- merhorn and his " six hundred" had compounded for the nation with the President and Senate, the nation con- tinued peacefully to struggle for their rights. In the winter of 1836 an effort was made for a new treaty. In July, 1837, a delegation was chosen to visit Washington. They presented their cause at the opening of Congress in a most able and lucid manner, sustained by the signa- tures of almost the whole Cherokee nation, and by nu- merous remonstrances from citizens of the United States. All was vain. No essential modification of the treaty could be effected. Still, they could not believe that a treaty which seemed to them so iniquitous and oppressive would be executed. And while the military were gath- ered round them, like the vultures round their victim, and while numerous fortifications were erected in the country, they remained quietly in their homes. Their grounds were planted for a larger crop than usual, when, on the 23d of May, 1838, the troops began to gather them from their cherished homes to the camps. Late in the season (August 19) the missionaries celebrated the Lord's Supper for the last time at Brainerd, and sixteen thou- sand people soon bade a mournful and reluctant adieu to the lands of their fathers. A five months' journey was before them. Sick and well, old man and infant, mothers and mothers that were to be, through the winter months they traveled on, from six to eighteen miles a day. There were births and there were deaths — but the deaths, alas! were two to one. They averaged thirteen deaths a day. They arrived at last; but more than four thousand — more than one fourth of their whole number — in that ten months time they had left beneath the sod. This shocking mortality was not due to special ill-treatment, but inevitable in such a removal. They bore it, on the whole, patiently. Many of the companies had religious services on the way, and all showed the influence of the missionaries in the fact that no such outbreaks of resistance as the government anticipated took place. No wonder that " Indian blood" so far boiled up the next year as to bring to an untimely end the three men who had sold their nation. Major Ridge was waylaid and shot. John Ridge, his son, was taken from his bed and cut to pieces. Elias Boudinot was decoyed from his house and slain with knives and hatchets. But John Ross and his friends expressed the deepest regret at such transactions, while the United States officers scoured the country in vain for the murderers. Aside from this, the deportment of the Cherokees, under their terrible trial, was worthy of a Christian people. And when men say the Indians can not be civilized and Christianized, posterity will sadly judge which party displayed the higher type of Christian manhood — John Ross and the Cherokee nation, or Andrew Jackson, Lewis Cass, the Reverend Commissioner Schermerhorn, Congressmen Coffee and Schley, Governor Lumpkin, Colonel Nelson, the Georgia Guard, the Georgia Legislature, and, must we add, the Senate of the United States in 1835. These things are facts of record ; on record let them stand.

But the palmy days of Indian missions were past for a generation. The shock of these events, and of the broad scheme to which it belonged, agitated and affected every tribe in the country. The little remnant of the Stockbridges were, for years, distressed by the question of a new removal. The Indians of New York were kept in a state of bitter complaint and internal dissension.

The remainder of this story may as well be briefly dispatched. It was almost a harvest of disasters, springing from one common root. The incoming flood of white and Indian corruption among the Chickasaws compelled the abandonment of that mission in 1834. The Osages, in 1836, made it positively unsafe to remain. In the same year the Creeks, instigated by neighboring whites with slanderous charges, petitioned the United States agent to remove the missionaries; and they were summarily expelled, without a hearing. In the discouragement of long-continued and still unsettled removal agitations, attended with a steady downward movement, the last missionary among the Stockbridges withdrew in 1848, and left them to a native pastor, Jeremiah Slingerland. The relics of the Tuscaroras in New York, with many of the marks and some of the vices of civilization, were left to themselves in 1860, having a church of a hundred members, and, for a time, the partial services of Peter P. Osunkirhine, a preacher of the Abenaqui tribe. In the Choctaw nation the influences of religion, never so thoroughly established, had been unfavorably affected by removal. The nation had recovered, in good degree, from the diminutions and the losses of removal; but they had learned from their former oppressors to enact stringent laws in defense of slavery. Some of these laws directly conflicted with the liberty of teaching and preaching. On the principles that should govern, and the methods that should be pursued in the circumstances, an important diversity of sentiment arose between the missionaries on the one side, and the Prudential Committee, the Board, and its patrons on the other. By reason of these embarrassments the mission was, in the year 1859, discontinued. At that time there were twelve churches, containing thirteen hundred and sixty-two members, of whom a small number, some twenty or thirty, perhaps, were holders of slaves. The Cherokee nation at this time numbered about twenty-one thousand. Our missionary work among them had never resumed its former importance, the four churches numbering only about two hundred communicants. But the Baptists, Moravians, and Methodists had largely entered. Meanwhile the nation had become, though with serious drawbacks, a " nominally Christian nation." For this alleged reason, re-enforced, no doubt, by other grave considerations, the mission was, in 1860, discontinued. The Seneca mission, in New York, was transferred to the Presbyterian Board in 1870, with the tribe increased one third in number (from twenty-five hundred in 1818 to thirty-three hundred and eighty-three in 1870), with houses finished and furnished, and lands cultivated, and their persons dressed like their white neighbors, with the district school system in full operation, and a record of six or seven hundred hopeful conversions during the history of the mission.

Rev. S. L. Hobbs, M. D., a missionary among the Choctaws many years ago, was urged to resume his labors among the people who had constituted his former charge ; and so earnest was their plea that the Prudential Committee authorized him to comply with their request.

He arrived at Fort Smith, on the border of the Indian Territory, in November, 1872. His field was very large, and its necessities were very great, partly because of the distressing demoralization which our civil war had caused, and partly because of the lack of any effective evangelistic agency during the ten previous years.

But the Lord was pleased to bless his labors, so that when he felt constrained to surrender his commission (June 1, 1876), he left behind him four churches, " well organized," and under the care of a native brother, who had been his pupil at Lenox before the war, but had secured ordination, and was supported by the Board of Missions of the Southern Presbyterian Church. The number of persons admitted to Christian fellowship during this brief period exceeded one hundred ; and others were expected to avail themselves of the same privilege at an early day. In addition to this spiritual fruitage, relief had been freely administered to the sick ; a marked impulse had been given to the temperance reform, — an object of exceptional importance among the aborigines of this country ; and many other benefits had been conferred upon the Choctaws. The Board has abundant reason, therefore, to be grateful for the privilege of accomplishing so much, with so small an expenditure.

The Dakota mission, the only remaining inheritance of the Board among the native tribes, deserves a separate description.

BARTLETT'S SKETCHES.

MISSIONS AMONG THE NORTH AMERICAN INDIANS. — THE DAKOTAS.

IN the year 1835 the Sioux, or more properly Dakota, Indians were one of the most powerful tribes on the continent, numbering, probably, from forty-five to fifty thousand. Their vast hunting-grounds extended from the forty-third to the forty-ninth degree of latitude, and from the Mississippi to the Black Hills west of the Missouri. The great State of Minnesota now occupies their eastern borders; and only a few years have passed since they were the sole occupants of Winona, Red Wing, and the region about St. Paul. It was within a few miles of one of the first missionary stations, near Fort Snelling, that Longfellow found a name which he has made famous. Minnehaha is a Dakota word, and means "Curling Water." A little stream plunges a precipice of sixty feet in a parabolic curve, and goes on its way, "curling along in laughing, childish glee," to join the Father of Waters. The name Dakota, "*alliance*," indicates the numerous bands that unite to form the tribe.

As early as the year 1834, two adventurous young Christian brothers from Connecticut, Samuel W. and Gideon II. Pond, pushed their way to Fort Snelling, joined a neighboring Indian village, built a log cabin, and applied themselves to learn the language, while in various

23

ways they made themselves useful to the natives. They afterward became ministers and missionaries of the Board, and their location seems to have determined one of the first two missionary stations, which was at Lake Harriet. One year later the American Board took up the work, sending the Revs. T. S. Williamson and J. D. Stevens, and the farmer Alexander Huggins, with their wives, and two unmarried ladies, Miss Stevens and Miss Poage. They were soon re-enforced by Rev. S. R. Riggs and wife, and the Messrs. Pond, with other lady teachers, and in later times by the children of the earlier missionaries.

The rough savage whom the missionaries found was quite a different person from the sentimental red man of the romance and the poem. The only poetic thing about the Dakota was the kind of religious maze — or muddle — in which he lived, whereby everything was *wakan*, or mysterious. So abundantly did the *takoo-wakan*, or the supernatural and mysterious, protrude itself through all nature and life, making gods innumerable, as to constitute almost a pantheism, or rather a pan-diabolism ; for " heaven and earth were full of demons, rankling with hate, and engaged in eternal strife ; " and " dread of future evil filled the souls " of the Dakotas. One " Great Spirit," omnipotent and all-pervading, so far at least as this tribe is concerned, is not so much an Indian belief as a white man's dream. Their chief gods were the most grotesque conceptions. The water god, or gods, rather, mightiest of all, one of whom dwelt in an iron den under the Falls of St. Anthony, in the form of a prodigious ox, with horns and tail expansible to the skies, the organs of power ; the thunder gods, of bird-like form, but terrible and hideous proportions, with double or quadruple-jointed wings, and of four varieties, black, yellow, scarlet, and blue, — the last of them globular in shape, without eyes or ears, and with eyebrows made of lines of lightning, hanging down in long, zigzag chains, — all dwelling in a palace, sentineled on its four sides by a butterfly, a bear, a reindeer, and a beaver, enveloped in scarlet down ; the moving god, dwelling in a boulder and in the four winds, as hard-hearted as the one, and as capricious as the other ; the anti-natural god, in four varieties, one of which carries a huge drum, using as a drumstick a thunder god, whom he holds by the tail, shivering with cold in hot weather, and fanning himself, naked, when the mercury congeals, bold in danger, and terrified in safety, with good for his evil, and evil for his good ; and so on, in infinite inconsistency and hopeless confusion.

Their religious rites and worship were worthy of the hideous beings they worshiped.   Streaked with blue and red paint, the Dakota performed his holiest services. He offered sacrifices to his gods (and to the spirits of the dead) from a piece of cloth or a kettle, a portion of every animal killed in the chase, or that greatest luxury of the Indian's own palate, dog-meat, up to the self-immolation, wherein, somewhat like the Hindu, the Indian cuts beneath the muscles of his breast, arms, and back, and suspends himself, by ropes passed through the incisions, to the top of a pole, for two or three days together, without food or drink.   He has religious dances and feasts, in one of which the worshipers howl round a great kettle of boiling meat, seizing the hot meat and devouring it, and then having the hot water thrown upon their legs ; and in another of which they dance round a pile of raw fish, till suddenly inspired, as they say, by the spirit of a

s

cormorant, they rush upon the fishes, tear them in pieces, and eat them down, scales, bones, entrails, and all. Sorcery and jugglery go naturally together.

The modern so-called spiritualism or spiritism of the white man is an old story with the Dakota Indians. They practiced summoning the spirits of the dead, and eliciting information concerning distant relatives and friends, all the while according to the most approved white man's mode, sitting with the fire-light extinguished, their blankets over their heads and singing in a low key, till the spirit comes with his "hair-erecting" disclosure. Indeed, the lofty feat wherein the Davenport brothers have, by twenty years' practice, acquired such expertness, tying and untying rope-knots in the dark, is, in all its important features, only the domestication of an ancient Dakota trick. Thus the juggler Red Bird, bound with ropes so tight as to break the skin, then tied, feet and hands together, and the whole body enveloped in knots and twists, with a buffalo robe fastened over all, was rolled into a tent, the lights extinguished, and all observers withdrawn. The tent is filled with rattlings, drummings, and voices. When at length the torches are lighted, Red Bird has slipped out of the robe and out of his fastenings, and left all the knots still tied.

There was little romance in Dakota life. It was hard on the men, and harder on the women. Bark wigwams were for summer, and the winter home was a conical-spreading tent, made of dressed buffalo-skins, supported by a framework of poles. A hole at the bottom let in the Indian, and a hole at the top let out the smoke. A coating of hay on the ground, covered partly by skin mats, with a central space left for the fire, formed floor and bed. Here, in bad weather, men, women, and boys sat and smoked. The women cut the fire-wood, dug the *tepsinna* root, dressed the buffalo-skins, cultivated the corn-patch, and packed and often carried the tent. The men did the hunting, fishing, fighting, and lounging. Food was precarious. After a hunt, meat was abundant. At other times, especially on a journey, they were reduced to great hardships, and went to bed "empty." Mr. Gideon Pond, on such an expedition, had the pleasure of regaling himself with otter, turtles, ground-nuts, and muskrats, while his copper-colored friends pronounced some dead fish, found on the lake shore, to be "good;" and Mr. S. W. Pond once saw some "hickory chips which had been boiled to get nourishment." When the former gentleman was feasted on turtle-soup, his appetite was reduced by having witnessed the turtles boiled alive in the savory mess, and by seeing a friendly squaw, as a special courtesy, wipe out his dish first with grass from beneath the floor-mat, and secondly with the corner of the short gown she had worn, day and night, all winter.

The tribe were not without their amusements, gay or grave. Their dances were varied enough for a more civilized race; six or seven in number, and crowned by the hideous scalp-dance. The great national game was ball, on which they bet as high as white men, staking not only their trinkets and equipments, but their horses, and sometimes their women. They had their more quiet games, their "plum-stones," partly answering the purpose of dice, and their "moccasin" game, — not exactly a compound of "button" and "hunt the slipper." The tooting of a rude flute or flageolet, and the pounding of a rattling, one-headed drum, or tambourine, sometimes enlivened the smoky wigwam of a winter evening or a stormy day.

The language was troublesome to the missionaries.

It not only abounded in clicks, and gutturals, and unpre-
cedented compositions, splitting a verb with a pronoun
or a preposition, but, like other heathen languages, it
was sadly defective for the utterance of religious ideas.
A " good heart" was but joy ; a " bad heart," grief; and
a "hard heart," courage. The *Wakan-Tanka*, or " Great
Spirit," was but an inferior god. The language was, of
course, unwritten, and imperfectly known. Sixteen years
from the commencement of the mission saw the publication
of a grammar, and a dictionary of fifteen thousand words.

In the midst of this degradation, the mission families
sent by the Board quietly and hopefully took up their
abode, in 1835, at two stations, — at Lake Harriet, near
Fort Snelling and the Falls of St. Anthony, and at
Lacquiparle, two hundred miles further west. Their
good work began even at Fort Snelling, where they
organized a church, and received eight new converts,
connected with the garrison, together with six members
of other churches. The very first year, at Lacquiparle,
brought in seven Dakota converts, and the second winter
nine, the third year ten, till, in six years, forty-nine
persons had been received.

The missionaries found, at Lacquiparle, a fast friend
and invaluable helper in Joseph Renville. He was the
son of a French father and a Dakota mother. Born in
a wigwam, and educated from his tenth year in Canada,
he had worked his way up from a trader's " runner "
and Indian " brave " to be an interpreter, a British captain, and agent of John Jacob Astor's American Fur
Company. He had now gained a commanding influence
in the Dakota nation, — an influence which he steadily
used for the benefit of the Indian, the traveler, and the
missionary. In a journey of seven hundred miles, from

Fort Snelling to the British posts, his ever open mansion was the one welcome resting-place. He furnished the missionaries a temporary home, and became at once their singularly sagacious and competent interpreter of the Scriptures. From the first, when Mr. Williamson wanted a chapter to read in meeting, he went to Mr. Renville for a translation. A little later, in 1837, there was from time to time a pleasant sight to be seen in his reception-room. In front of a roaring fire sat Mr. Renville at his ease, and at a table near, with books and writing materials, sat Messrs. Williamson, Riggs, and G. H. Pond. A verse was read aloud from the French Bible, repeated by Mr. Renville in Dakota, and written down by the missionaries. Thus they went through the gospels of Mark and John. Mr. Renville's interest in the missionaries was not without its reward. His Indian wife was the first full-blooded Dakota convert, and the first that died in the faith. He himself became a worthy and consistent elder in the church, while one of his sons and one or more of his grandsons became preachers of the gospel.

For some years the accessions to the church were mostly women. Their obstacles were less than those of the men. The change involved far less revolution of dress, habits, life, and pursuit; drew less attention and less opposition. To the man, it meant complete reversal and reconstruction, outward as well as inward, from the cutting of his long hair, and the putting on of decent apparel, to the abandonment of polygamy; from the " scalp-dance" to the scalping expedition. Meekness of spirit and industry of life were hard sayings to an Indian brave. But in the end, the word and Spirit of God proved equal to the work.

From the first there were lovely spirits developed in those rude bodies. There was Hapanna, at Lake Calhoun, long enduring, all alone, not only the social opposition and persecution of her whole band, but from her own husband slanders, threats, beatings, dangerous wounds, and final abandonment; yet living and dying in the faith, and followed to heaven by her once abusive husband. There was Lightning-Face, wife of Pine-Shooter, once ragged and dirty, and a heathen so zealous as to forbid her children attending the meetings, hide their moccasons, and leave them to go barefoot in the snow, yet led by the Spirit to embrace the gospel with a wonderfully firm and child-like faith. And when, one summer morning, in 1867, a flash of lightning called her away, none doubted she had gone to be with God, where her husband had gone before. There was Catharine Brown, willing to be put away as the second wife; submitting to the cutting up of her blanket, and other similar trials; keeping the Sabbath, even though it entailed separation from her traveling company; learning to read, spin, knit, and weave, and entering into every plan for her people's elevation; bringing up her children for the Lord, and holding fast the faith in a good old age. There were Christian children, like Jenny Simon, weeping over her sins, and giving her heart to Christ when eleven years old, and passing away at fourteen, with such words on her lips as these: " I love all my friends here, but I love Jesus more." These, and many like cases, proved from the first the old, but ever new, transforming power of the gospel.

The life of the missionaries was not destitute of adventures. Mr. S. W. Pond barely escaped perishing on a trip from Lake Harriet to Lacquiparle. Overtaken by a storm, losing his way, benumbed with cold, four days fasting, mistrustful of the gun of his Indian guide, a stray horse bore him exhausted to his destination, and saved his life. Dr. Williamson passed one winter in fear of starvation, the young men who went for his winter's supply having been compelled to abandon all, and almost perished on the way. On one occasion Mr. and Mrs. Hopkins and Mrs. Riggs encountered an Ojibwa war-party with two fresh Dakota scalps, and just afterward the still more dangerous party of excited Dakotas, who laid the blame of the murder upon the missionaries, and killed one of their horses on the spot. The terrified women pursued their way on foot, under a burning sun, comforting their hearts with those same words with which the Georgia colonel had once taunted the Cherokee missionaries: "Fear not, little flock." Mr. Riggs was once a "mark for an Indian arrow," and again "chased by the scalping-knife in the hands of a drunken man."

These were stray shots. At length came something of the grapple that is almost inevitable in the history of missions to the heathen. When the gospel began fairly to take hold of the Indian warriors, their chiefs and braves set themselves to stop it. They frightened away the children and broke up the schools, in some cases for months together. They posted guards to prevent attendance on Sabbath worship, and cut up the blankets of those who persisted. In more than one instance men who had embraced or favored the new religion died suddenly and mysteriously, and there was talk of "bad medicine," — the witchcraft of ancient and of modern times. Sometimes they used the methods of the tempter. Simon, one of the bravest of the braves, had become a Christian.

For four years he nobly stood the scorn of all his associates, and the very hootings of the children as he went
abroad, that Simon was a woman now. But another
band tried friendship and flattery. They invited him to
their dog-feasts, praised his prowess, and treated him to
" spirit-water." He fell, repented, fell, repented again,
and fell deeper. For some years he stood aloof. He
was followed by prayers and persuasions. He would
listen, promise, and slink away. At length he came and
sat on the church doorstep, but would not enter. In
1854 all the mission buildings at Lacquiparle, except the
church, burned down. It was the signal for Simon's
full and final return. He was restored to his standing,
honored his profession, stood by the mission in the hour
of its fiery trial, and became at length a preacher of the
gospel.

But not all the tempted were thus recovered; and
strong drink was one of the chief temptations. There
was a time, in 1849, when many of the schools were
shut up, the attendance at religious meetings very small,
two fifths of the church members in a state of defection,
the mission almost disabled by the stealing of their
property and the constant killing of their cattle, a war
raging between the Dakotas and the Ojibwas, and the
country flooded with strong drink. Still it did not prevent the formation of two little churches in 1850. Then
came the protracted excitement of treaties and cessions
to the United States, the influx of settlers and specula-
tors in village sites and city lots. But now also came
the happy influence of the missionary work on the destinies of Minnesota; for the men who carried the gospel
to the aborigines, also aided in forming the religious
institutions of the white settlers. Four members of

the mission, indeed, withdrew to engage in the home service.

Meanwhile new Indian churches were organized at Yellow Medicine and Redwood, the one at Lacquiparle being transferred to Hazelwood; and when the treaty excitement had passed away, the field seemed more hopeful than ever. In 1856 was formed the " Hazelwood Republic," with a written constitution, and all the methods of a Christian civilization. It was followed by a similar one at Redwood. The chapel at Yellow Medicine had been built without cost to the Board. The little church at Redwood was often filled to overflowing, and the clear-toned bell at Hazelwood often summoned near a hundred worshipers. The Indians built them log, and frame, and — with government aid — brick houses, and began to raise grain, and other farm products, for sale.

But now drew nigh the time that tried the faith and tested the work of the missionaries. Opposers had said that the mission was a failure, and that the Christian Indians were more hostile to the whites than were the pagans. God signally branded the falsehood. But he did it, as it could only be done, in scenes of fire and blood.

There was a premonition as early as 1857. A white settlement of six or eight families, on the beautiful cluster of waters called Spirit Lake, lay near the hunting range of the chief Scarlet End. The winter was snowy, and hunting unproductive. The Indians, after annoying the settlers all around, came to an open rupture at Spirit Lake. They killed forty persons, and carried off the cattle, clothing, and provisions, and four captive women. One of the women was killed at the Sioux River because she could not cross it upon a log, and another afterward in the Indian camp; the third was

purchased, and restored to her friends, by two sons of
the early convert Rebekah, and the fourth was recovered
by the courage and skill of three Indian messengers.
Great excitements and alarms attended the ineffectual
attempts of the government to bring the offenders to
justice. At one time Dr. Williamson saw the conical
tents of five thousand warriors on the prairie between
him and the camp of Major Sherman. The escape of
Scarlet End and his assassins was not forgotten.

Five years passed away. The United States was
fairly locked in its great struggle with the southern
rebellion. The heathen portion of the Dakotas, stimu-
lated by their medicine men and war prophets, had long
been growing bitter toward Christianity and civilization,
and watched their opportunity. Said they to Mr. Potter,
" We do not desire your instruction ; we wish you gone."
The government and the traders had badly compromised
Christian civilization. Of the general course of the
government agents, and the traders to these Indians, it
is but historic justice to say that it had been one long-
continued imposition and outrage. The traders sold
them goods at enormous prices, plunged them in debt,
drugged them with spirits, and debauched their women.
The traders and the government steadily played into
each other's hands. It was the old fable, true at last, of
the lion and the jackal. When a cession of lands was
to be procured, the traders lent themselves, by fair
means and by foul, to bring it about. They threatened
loss of trade and of credit on the one hand, they held
out the most delusive expectations on the other, and
they procured the signatures of the Indians, on false
pretenses, to contracts and vouchers not explained nor
understood. When the money came, the government

agents paid, first of all, the claims of these traders ; and " most of the money due under these treaties," says one who had investigated, " went into the hands of government officials, traders, and other swindlers." * The government had a way, too, of " breaking chiefs " when necessary, and, as Red Iron said to Governor Ramsay, of " having boys made chiefs to sign papers, and getting single chiefs to council at night to be bribed to sign papers." In one instance four hundred thousand dollars were paid by the government directly to the traders on old indebtedness, of which one Hugh Tyler received (in 1857) fifty-five thousand dollars for getting treaties through the Senate and through the chiefs. Nor were the stipulations about schools and implements carried out. " The treaties," says the writer above quoted, " are born of fraud, and all their stipulations curtailed by iniquity." †

These general exasperations were, in 1862, embittered by fresh grievances. In the previous year the government at Washington had made an arrangement to change their money annuity to goods, which made the payment at the proper time impossible. In July five thousand Sissetons came for their money. It was not ready, nor even promised them. Pinched with hunger, and some of them dying of starvation, they broke into the warehouse, helped themselves, and went home. The agent was thoroughly frightened for the time. A little later some of the traders not only refused the Indians credit, but insulted them by telling them they " might starve or eat dirt." It was close upon the outbreak.

---

* Heard's History of the Sioux War, p. 42.
† Ib., p. 33.

Rumors of fighting came up from the rebellion, and acted like the distant smell of blood upon a wolf. The Indians kept hearing that their " Great Father was whipped." They saw that whites and half-breeds were invited to enlist. The able-bodied men of the white settlements were away to the war. Now was the opportunity. The prudence of the old chiefs was overridden by the fierce counsels of the young braves, and they determined to carry desolation through all the settlements of Minnesota, and seize again the hunting-grounds of their fathers.

The tinder was all laid when the spark fell. At Acton, four Indians, first roused by a mutual quarrel, then ejected from a house after a contention with the owner about liquor and a gun, and called " black devils" by his wife at a neighbor's, suddenly shot them and three other persons, and hurried away to their band with the story. All felt it to be an irretrievable step. Next morning, early, a hundred and fifty armed and mounted Indians throng round the house of Little Crow, all eager for a fray. The old chief sits up in bed, and great beads of sweat stand on his forehead. He sees the peril, for he had been in Washington. But the die is cast. His hopes and fears at home, and the excitement of the hour, force him on. "I am with you. Let us go to the agency, kill the traders, and take their goods." Deacon Paul and John Otherday boldly resisted in council, at peril of their lives, but in vain. They then rescued the white families, conferred with the troops, organized opposition, and afterward delivered the prisoners.

Little Crow and his vultures hurried to the lower agency, near Redwood, the same day, surrounded the houses and stores in small squads, and on the firing of

the signal gun at the store where first they were told to
" eat dirt," they commenced an indiscriminate slaughter.
When the horrid work was finished here, they scattered
to spread it through the country. Messengers were sent
to the upper Indians, and numerous bands engaged in
the massacre.

It was the evening of the 18th of August that word
came to Hazelwood of the slaughter, forty miles away,
and of a band of fifty soldiers, hastening to the spot,
driven back, with the loss of half their number, and
all their arms. After dark strange faces were seen
flitting round the mission, and the property began to
disappear. Larger bands came passing by, and Simon
and Paul hastened the mission family away. At mid-
night a company of twenty persons might have been seen
stealing to the woods in the rear, guided and aided by
Indian friends. It was Mr. Riggs and his company.
They were paddled across the Minnesota, followed by an
Indian woman with a forgotten bag of provisions. Then
they crawled through the ravines to the prairie. Here
they joined the company of Mr. Williamson, who had
lived two miles away. For a week they plodded on together, through driving rains and long, wet swamp grass,
exhausted, and often hungry. The children, as they
crawled under the wagons, out of the rain, at night, cried
for " home ; " and the young traveling bride from New
Jersey thought in the morning " they might as well die
as live." They crossed several trails of the murderers,
and little knew that one savage party was on their own
trail, but was misled by their friend Peter Bigfire. They
came in sight of Fort Ridgely ; but it was sending up
rocket-signals of distress, and they went on, by an escape
so narrow that four men who left their company were

T

killed an hour after, within hearing of the guns. They reached St. Paul in safety, just as the dispatch had come from New Jersey to recover the bodies of the young bride and her husband.

On the same morning, when these left Hazelwood and Redwood, another company of sixty-two left Yellow Medicine. Honest John Otherday was their guide and protector. With the chances of escape, as he said, " one in a thousand," he brought them all safe to St. Paul; " and," said he, " my heart is glad." Simon, too, the relapsed and recovered Simon, proved true as steel. Leaving his own family to shift for themselves, he brought Mrs. Newman and her three children to Fort Ridgely, he and his son hiding in the day time and travelling by night. Five weeks later, a hundred captive women and children were found at " Camp Release," also rescued by the loyal Indians, by purchase or persuasion.

But long before this Little Crow and his horde had done their work. With torch and tomahawk they had swept an area of twenty thousand miles, — fifteen or twenty border counties. They had killed some six or seven hundred persons, burnt the mission premises, and the houses of all the Christian Indians, pressed Forts Ridgely and Abercrombie, and defeated a detachment of two hundred troops. In the horrors they committed the savages outdid themselves, and relapsed into fiends. They tortured the living, and offered every conceivable indignity and insult to the dead. They cut off the hands, feet, and heads of their victims, and tore out their hearts. They roasted an infant in an oven, spared not even the unborn, nailed children to tables and doors, thrêw their knives and tomahawks at them, and amused themselves by shooting arrows at women and children. One wretch killed seven children in one wagon. Still fouler wrongs were inflicted on captive women, to an incredible extent, ended sometimes by natural death, and once at least by the horrid torture of impalement. These murders and tortures of women and children were mostly the work of the younger braves, against the advice of their chief.

For three weeks they carried all before them. The Christian party put forth a bold and powerful influence to resist and divide their counsels, and formed a camp for self-protection At length a body of twelve hundred United States troops pushed up the Minnesota Valley, routed the forces of Little Crow at Wood Lake, and finally scattered them to the west and north.

The leaders and the most guilty escaped. Little Crow fled, appropriately, to Devil's Lake. In the following July, near the town of Hutchinson, an Indian was shot while picking berries in the woods. His height and his grayish hair, his teeth, double all round, his left arm withered, and his right arm once broken and badly set, marked him as Little Crow, the foremost orator and hunter of the Sioux Indians. His skeleton, we believe, adorns the rooms of an Historical Society.

Four or five hundred men fell into the hands of our troops, by capture or voluntary surrender. The government was now resolved to punish; but the work was overdone. A military commission tried four hundred men in one month, dispatching them at the rate, sometimes, of thirty or forty in a day, and, of course, on very summary grounds. Fifty were acquitted, twenty sentenced to imprisonment, and more than three hundred condemned to be hung. President Lincoln was wiser than the military commission. He ordered that sentence of death be executed only on those who were proved guilty of individual murders or of rape. On that finding, thirty-eight Dakotas were hung in one day. Only three of them could read, and none of them had ever attended a mission school. Three hundred and thirty remained in prison at Mankato.

And here were unfolded the strange plans and methods of God. The prisoners were broken and humbled. Eight or ten of them could read and write. Dr. Williamson and his sister distributed among them slates, paper, and pencils. As the readers and writers began to while away the time, their example became contagious, and soon the whole prison was a school-house. They wrote to their families at Camp Snelling, and that, too, became a school. On a visit made in March, 1863, Mr. Riggs carried some four hundred letters from the camp to the prison, and about as many back to the camp. The Indians lost confidence in their gods, and listened more earnestly to the gospel. By a notable providence, among them was Robert Hopkins Chaskay, an elder in the church at Yellow Medicine. He had been caught hanging foolishly round the scene of havoc, with his gun, which he fired at an ox, and was condemned to death. By special efforts of the missionaries his sentence was commuted. He was thus in prison, to coöperate within with the missionaries without.

A great revival took place in the prison that winter, and in the spring two hundred Dakotas were added to the church in one day; and when the government transferred the prisoners by steamer to Davenport, they passed St. Paul in chains, indeed, but singing the fifty-first psalm, to the tune of Old Hundred. The good work spread at the same time, as by electric induction, into their families, and went on in the prison at Davenport. It was not till 1866 that the prisoners were released and joined their families, then at Niobrara in Nebraska. All the professors of religion, now numbering four hundred, chose to be gathered at first into the one " Pilgrim Church." Next year a long step forward was taken, in the choice of two native pastors, and the licence of two other native preachers of the gospel.

And now was inaugurated in the Dakota mission, — although on a more limited scale, — substantially the same policy which was about the same time begun in Central Turkey, of falling back upon the home agency, — apostolic missionaries and native pastors. The mission had now reached the stage where this course was possible. No eye but that of God could have seen, in the great Indian uprising and massacre, the opening of a new missionary expansion. When the missionaries fled from Hazelwood, Miss Martha Riggs wrote in her journal, " The feeling came over us that our life-work had been in vain." The Lord seeth not as man seeth. It was but the opening of a new era.

Since then the prosperity of the business has gone steadily forward, the Lord working marvelously with them for his own name's sake, till, in 1871, the mission was able to report nine stations and out-stations, and eight churches, containing more than seven hundred members, — one hundred of them received during the year. Mr. Riggs is now aided in the good work by two sons, (the younger having gone to Fort Sully in February, 1872), and a daughter, and Mr. Williamson by his son; while Joseph Renville, though dead, preaches the gospel by his son and his grandson. Six pastors, four licen-

tiates, and three teachers, all natives, are aiding the
missionaries, and planting permanent institutions. Two
training-schools are raising up more helpers. A Dakota
newspaper is binding the churches together. Three
thousand Indians are said to have embraced a civilized
life, and the influences of civilization have more or less
been brought to bear on ten thousand more. Some of
them have renounced all tribal relations and allegiance,
and all expectation of sharing in the annuities, that they
may become citizens of the United States, own their individual homesteads, and stand on the plane of full civilized manhood. The churches are doing much toward
the support of their own institutions. There is increasing
willingness to hear the gospel in new fields; young men
come from a distance to school; and the missionaries
and native pastors are steadily pushing forth in new ex-
plorations, with much encouragement. A station is at
once to be occupied at Fort Sully, three hundred miles
beyond the Santee agency, among the "wild" Indians
on the Upper Missouri. It is also a gratifying fact that
the tribe, and particularly the more civilized portion,
is steadily increasing. The government policy seems
to have changed at last. Congress has taken up an
apparently resolute inquiry into the colossal frauds that
are perpetrated upon the aborigines of this country, and
while this sketch is writing, President Grant has declared
"his purpose to see that all the rights and interests of
the Indians are protected." If this new policy can but
be adhered to, and faithfully executed, and should the
present missionary movement be suffered to go on without interference, there is reason to hope that the great
problem of Indian Christianization, civilization, and
preservation, will at last be effectually solved.

About the time this sketch was first published (1872), Rev. T. S. Williamson, M. D., and his son, Rev. John P. Williamson, transferred their connection from the American Board to the Presbyterian Board of Foreign Missions. Somewhat more than one fourth of the native church membership they retained under their supervision; and in all matters involving a common expenditure, as in the publishing department, they agreed to bear one third, leaving two thirds to those who remained with the American Board. Notwithstanding this change, the Dakota Mission continues substantially as it was.

In the year 1871, an Annual Conference, consisting of all the churches, pastors, and missionaries, was inaugurated. This has been a bond of union and strength, as it brings together, at some point in the field, from year to year, the Christian workers, and gives them an opportunity for the interchange of sympathy, counsel, and help; the Holy Spirit has been manifestly present with them. This Conference at its last annual meeting took measures to organize a Native Foreign Mission Society, which, if consummated, will educate these Dakota Christians in the higher work of giving the Gospel to those who still sit in darkness.

During the last four years, considerable progress has been made in the various departments of work. The then new station near Fort Sully has become fully organized; and Rev. T. L. Riggs and wife, with two young lady assistants, are now occupying the main station at Bogue, and they have two out-stations, Hope and Chantier, which are manned by native teachers. At each of these three places there are flourishing schools, and the Gospel has been preached in the Teeton dialect, in the expectation of a spiritual harvest, when the " power from on high " shall be given.

The plans of Rev. A. L. Riggs, at the Santee Agency in Nebraska, have been partly developed. A plain but commodious building has been completed, and it is occupied as a girls' boarding school, called the Girls' Home. His training school for young men, for which he has no proper building as yet, has increased from year to year, and this last winter, for a short period, he added to it a theological class of half a dozen.

At the Yankton Agency, and in the Settlement on the Big Sioux, two new school and church buildings have been erected. And three of the churches on the Sissiton Reservation have built houses of worship, in part by their own efforts; while at the same time they have been increasing in their contributions for the support of their own pastors, and also for benevolent work.

The "Iapi Oaye," or "Word Carrier," is now in its fifth year, and has demonstrated its necessity by its extensive civilizing and Christianizing as well as unifying influences, upon the whole work. The schools, government and missionary, have greatly increased the number of readers. Books have been added to those which were in use before. A Model English-Dakota Reader, prepared by members of the mission, has been published, mainly at the expense of the government. A beautiful book in Elementary Geography, in Dakota, has issued from the press of Scribner, Armstrong, & Co. The Dakota Bible has received considerable additions during these four years; and a new edition will be published by the American Bible Society this year, containing the whole of the New Testament, and all the books of the Old from Genesis to Second Samuel inclusive, as also from the Psalms to Malachi.

For years the members of the Dakota mission have

been greatly interested in the Indian community at. Fort Berthold, on the Upper Missouri. The three remnants of tribes, living together in one village, the Mandans, the Rees, and Gros Ventres or Hidatsa, are not Dakotas, (though two of them belong to the Dakota language family.) But such has been their connection with our government and people for the last century, that their civilization and Christianization have seemed to become a matter of unquestionable obligation. The Lord has now opened the way for the occupancy of that distant post. Rev. Charles L. Hall, and Mrs. Emma C. Hall, under a commission from the American Board, left the Yankton Agency by a Missouri steamer, April 26, 1876. God giving them prosperity, the station may be regarded as occupied, and an additional appeal may go forth to the Christian people of the land for help, through their sympathies, and their prayers, and their contributions.

Including Fort Berthold station in the Dakota mission, as also the Presbyterian part of it, there are five stations, ten out-stations, eight ordained native ministers, two licentiates, and several students in theology, eight native churches, with an aggregate membership of about 800.

MISSIONARIES OF THE AMERICAN BOARD, 1876.

MISSIONARIES.	Began their labors.
Rev. S. R. Riggs	1837
Mrs. Annie B. Riggs	1872
Rev. Alfred L. Riggs	1870
Mrs. Mary B. Riggs	1870
Mr. Wyllys K. Morris	1870
Mrs. Martha Riggs Morris	1870
Rev. Thomas L. Riggs	1872

Mrs. Nina F. Riggs	1873
Miss Maria L. Haines	1874
Miss Martha A. Shepard	1875
Miss Mary C. Collins	1875
Miss Emmie Whipple	1875
Mrs. Adele M. Curtis	1875
Miss Lucy Dodge	1876
Rev. Charles L. Hall	1876
Mrs. Emma C. Hall	1876

General Summary.

The following resumé will show how *many* Indian tribes the Board has embraced in its plans, for *how long a period*, with *what agency*, as also, in part, with *what results*.

(*a.*) *Cherokees.* — 1816–60. One hundred and thirteen missionaries, mostly lay and female. Twelve churches and 248 members in 1860. Schools. Printing, 14,084,-100 pages. Given up because the proper work of the Board was supposed to be done.

(*b.*) *Choctaws.* — 1818–59. One hundred and fifty-three missionaries, including lay and female. Twelve churches and 1,362 members in 1859. Schools. Printing, 11,588,000 pages. Given up because of complications arising from the existence of slavery. One missionary resumed labor in 1872, and withdrew in 1876, leaving four churches in the care of a native pastor.

(*c.*) *Osages.* — 1826–37. Twenty-six missionaries. Two churches of 48 members. Large schools of 354 scholars. Their country ceded to the Cherokees.

(*d.*) *Maumee.* — 1826–35. Six missionaries. A church of 25 members. Given up because of changes in the population.

(*e.*) *Mackinaw.* — 1826–36. Seventeen missionaries. A church of 35 members. Given up as above.

(*f.*) *Chickasaws.* — 1827–35. Ten missionaries. A church at one time of 100 members and schools containing 300 pupils. Given up as above.

(*g.*) *Stockbridge.* — 1828–48. Eight missionaries. A church of 51 members. Given up as above.

(*h.*) *Creeks.* — 1832–37. Six missionaries. Eighty church members. Given up because of peculiar embarrassments not to be overcome.

(*i.*) *Pawnees.* — 1834–44. Ten missionaries. Given up because of the roving character of the Pawnees and the hostile incursions of other tribes.

(*j.*) *Oregon.* — 1835–47. Thirteen missionaries. Broken up by the massacre of 1847.

(*k.*) *Senecas.* — 1826–70. Forty-seven missionaries. Transferred to the Presbyterian Board in 1870. From first to last about 600 church members.

(*l.*) *Tuscaroras.* — 1826–60. Ten missionaries. Given up because the proper work of the Board was supposed to be done. From first to last about 200 church members.

(*m.*) *Ojibways.* — 1831–70. Twenty-eight missionaries. Transferred to the Presbyterian Board in 1870. Number of converts not definitely known.

(*n.*) *Dakotas.* — 1835– —. Forty missionaries. In part transferred to the Presbyterian Board in 1870. Not far from 1,000 church members from the first.

(*o.*) *Abenaquis.* — 1835–56. One Indian missionary. Given up because of increasing discouragements. Some 75 church members from the first.

Condensed Summary.

Twelve missions closed; 2⅓ transferred. Five hundred missionaries. Forty-five churches, 3,700 members. Schools and printing more or less in all. The whole number of Indians reached by these missions not far from 100,000.

HISTORICAL SKETCH

OF THE

MISSIONS OF THE AMERICAN BOARD

IN THE

SANDWICH ISLANDS, MICRONESIA, AND MARQUESAS.

BY

REV. S. C. BARTLETT, D. D.

BOSTON:
PUBLISHED BY THE BOARD,
1 SOMERSET STREET.
1876.

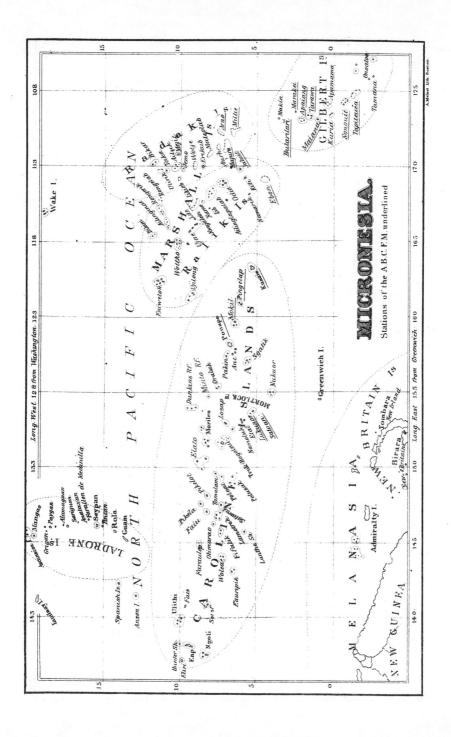

MICRONESIA.

Stations of the A.B.C.F.M. underlined

A.Meisel Lith. Boston.

BARTLETT'S SKETCHES.

THE SANDWICH ISLANDS, MICRONESIA, AND MARQUESAS.

In the year 1809, a dark-skinned boy was found weeping on the door-steps at Yale College. His name was Henry Obookiah (Opukahaia); and he came from the Sandwich Islands. In a civil war his father and mother had been slain before his eyes; and when he fled with his infant brother on his back, the child was killed with a spear, and he was taken prisoner. Lonely and wretched, the poor boy, at the age of fourteen, was glad to come with Captain Brintnell to New Haven. He thirsted for instruction; and he lingered round the college buildings, hoping in some way to gratify his burning desire. But when at length all hope died out, he sat down and wept. The Rev. Edwin W. Dwight, a resident graduate, found him there, and kindly took him as a pupil.

In the autumn of that year came another resident graduate to New Haven, for the purpose of awakening the spirit of missions. It was Samuel J. Mills. Obookiah told Mills his simple story — how the people of Hawaii " are very bad; they pray to gods made of wood;" and he longs " to learn to read this Bible, and go back there and tell them to pray to God up in heaven." Mills wrote to Gordon Hall, " What does this mean? Brother Hall, do you understand it? Shall he be sent back unsup-

1

ported, to attempt to reclaim his countrymen? Shall
we not rather consider these southern islands a proper
place for the establishment of a mission?" Mills took
Obookiah to his own home in Torringford, and thence
to Andover for a two years' residence; after which the
young man found his way to the Grammar School at
Litchfield, and, when it was opened in 1817, to the
Foreign Mission School at Cornwall, Conn. At Litchfield he became acquainted and intimate with Samuel
Ruggles, who, about this time (1816), resolved to accompany him to his native island with the gospel.

In the same vessel which brought Obookiah to Amer-
ica came two other Hawaiian lads, William Tenooe
(Kanui) and Thomas Hopu. After roving lives of many
years, in 1815 they were both converted — Tenooe at
New Haven, and Hopu after he had removed from New
Haven to Torringford. Said Hopu, after his conversion,
" I want my poor countrymen to know about Christ."
These young men, too, had been the objects of much
personal interest in New Haven; and in the following
June, during the sessions of the General Association in
that city, a meeting was called by some gentlemen to
discuss the project of a Foreign Mission School. An
organization was effected under the American Board that
autumn, at the house of President Dwight, three months
before his death. Next year the school opened. Its first
principal was Mr. Edwin W. Dwight, — who found Obookiah in tears at Yale College, — and among its first pupils
were Obookiah, Tenooe, Hopu, and two other Hawaiian
youths, with Samuel Ruggles and Elisha Loomis.

But Obookiah was never to carry the gospel in person
to his countrymen. God had a wiser use for him. In
nine months from the opening of the Mission School, he

closed a consistent Christian life with a peaceful Christian death. The lively interest which had been gathering round him was profoundly deepened by his end and the memoir of his life, and was rapidly crystallizing into a mission. Being dead, he yet spoke with an emphasis and an eloquence that never would have been given him in his life. The touching story drew legacies from the dying, and tears, prayers, donations, and consecrations from the living. " O, what a wonderful thing," he once had said, " that the hand of Divine Providence has brought me here from that heathenish darkness! And here I have found the name of the Lord Jesus in the Holy Scriptures, and have read that his blood was shed for many. My poor countrymen, who are yet living in the region and shadow of death! — I often feel for them in the night season, concerning the loss of their souls. May the Lord Jesus dwell in my heart, and prepare me to go and spend the remainder of my life with them. But not my will, but thine, O Lord, be done.'

The will of the Lord *was* done. The coming to America was a more " wonderful thing " than he thought. His mantle fell on other shoulders, and in two years more a missionary band was ready for the Sandwich Islands. Hopu, Tenooe, and John Honoree, natives of the islands, were to be accompanied by Hiram Bingham and Asa Thurston, young graduates of Andover, Dr. Thomas Holman, a young physician, Daniel Chamberlain, a substantial farmer, Samuel Whitney, mechanic and teacher, Samuel Ruggles, catechist and teacher, and Elisha Loomis, printer and teacher. All the Americans were accompanied by their wives, and Mr. Chamberlain by a family of five children. Mr. Ruggles seems to have been the first to determine upon joining the mission, and Mr.

Loomis had been a member of the Mission School. With this company went also George Tamoree (Kamaulii), who had been a wanderer in America for fourteen years, to return to his father, the subject king of Kauai.

The ordination of Messrs. Bingham and Thurston at Goshen, Conn., drew from the surrounding region a large assembly, among whom were a great number of clergymen, and nearly all the members of the Mission School, now thirty or more in number; and "liberal offerings" for the mission came in "from all quarters." A fortnight later the missionary band was organized at Boston into a church of seventeen members; public services were held Friday evening and Saturday forenoon in the presence of "crowded" houses, at the Park Street Church; and on the Sabbath six hundred communicants sat with them at the table of the Lord. "The occasion," says the "Panoplist" of that date, "was one of the most interesting and solemn which can exist in this world." On Saturday, the 23d of October, 1819, a Christian assembly stood upon Long Wharf, and sang, "Blest be the tie that binds." There was a prayer by Dr. Worcester, a farewell speech by Hopu, a song by the missionaries, "When shall we all meet again;" and a fourteen-oared barge swiftly conveyed the little band from their weeping friends to the brig Thaddeus, which was to carry the destiny of the Hawaiian Islands.

While the missionaries are on their way, let us take a look at the people whom they were going to reclaim. The ten islands of the Hawaiian group — an area somewhat less than Massachusetts — were peopled by a well-formed, muscular race, with olive complexions and open countenances, in the lowest stages of barbarism, sensuality, and vice. The children went stark naked till they were nine or ten years old ; and the men and women wore the scantiest apology for clothing, which neither sex hesitated to leave in the hut at home before they passed through the village to the surf.   The king came more than once from the surf to the house of Mr. Ruggles with his five wives, all in a state of nudity ; and on being informed of the impropriety, he came the next time dressed — with a pair of silk stockings and a hat !   The natives had hardly more modesty or shame than so many animals. Husbands had many wives, and wives many husbands, and exchanged with each other at pleasure.   The most revolting forms of vice, as Captain Cook had occasion to know, were practiced in open sight.   When a foreign vessel came to the harbor, the women would swim to it in flocks for the vilest of purposes.   Two thirds of all the children, probably, were destroyed in infancy — strangled or buried alive.

The nation practiced human sacrifice ; and there is a cord now at the Missionary Rooms, Chicago, with which one high priest had strangled twenty-three human victims. They were a race of perpetual thieves ; even kings and chiefs kept servants for the special purpose of stealing. They were wholesale gamblers, and latterly drunkards. Thoroughly savage, they seemed almost destitute of fixed habits.   When food was plenty, they would take six or seven meals a day, and even rise in the night to eat ; at other times they would eat but once a day, or perhaps go almost fasting for two or three days together.   And for purposes of sleep the day and the night were much alike. Science they had none ; no written language, nor the least conception of any mode of communicating thought but by oral speech.

A race that destroyed their own children had little

tender mercy. Sons often buried their aged parents
alive, or left them to perish. The sick were abandoned
to die of want and neglect. Maniacs were stoned to
death. Captives were tortured and slain. The whole
system of government and religion was to the last degree
oppressive. The lands, their products, and occupants
were the property of the chiefs and the king. The persons and power of the high chiefs were protected by a
crushing system of restrictions, called *tabus*. It was
tabu and death for a common man to let his shadow fall
upon a chief, to go upon his house, enter his enclosure,
or wear his *kapa*, to stand when the king's *kapa* or his
bathing water was carried by, or his name mentioned in
song. In these and a multitude of other ways, " men's
heads lay at the feet of the king and the chiefs." In like
manner it was tabu for a woman to eat with her husband,
or to eat fowl, pork, cocoa-nut, or banana, — things offered
to the idols, — and death was the penalty. The priest,
too, came in with his tabus and his exactions for his idols.
There were six principal gods with names, and an indefinite number of spirits. Whatsoever the priest demanded for the god — food, a house, land, human sacrifice — must be forthcoming. If he pronounced a day
tabu, the man who was found in a canoe, or even enjoy-
ing the company of his family, died. If any one made
a noise when prayers were saying, or if the priest pronounced him irreligious, he died. When a temple was
built, and the people had finished the toil, some of them
were offered in sacrifice. In all these modes, the oppression of the nation was enormous.

The race had once been singularly healthy. They told
the first missionaries — an exaggeration, of course — that
formerly they died only of old age. But foreign sailors

had introduced diseases, reputable, and especially dis-
reputable; and now, between the desolations of war, infanticide, and infamous diseases widely spread by general
licentiousness, the nation was rapidly wasting away.

Such was the forbidding race on whom the missionaries
were to try the power of the cross.   " Probably none of
you will live to witness the downfall of idolatry," — so
said the Rev. Mr. Kellogg to Mr. Ruggles, as they took
breakfast together at East Windsor, the morning before
he left home.   And so thought, no doubt, the whole community.   But God's thoughts are not as our thoughts.

Hopu called up his friend Ruggles at one o'clock on a
moonlight night (March 31), to get the first glimpse of
Hawaii; and at daybreak the snow-capped peak of
Mauna Kea was in full view.   A few hours more, and
Hopu pointed out the valley where he was born.   A boat
is put off, with Hopu and others in it, which encounters
some fishermen, and returns.   As the boat nears the vessel, Hopu is seen swinging his hat in the air; and as soon
as he arrives within hail, he shouts, " Oahu's idols are no
more ! "   On coming aboard, he brings the thrilling news
that the old king Kamehameha is dead; that Liholiho,
his son, succeeds him; that the images of the gods are
all burned; that the men are all " Inoahs," — they eat
with the women; that but one chief was killed in settling
the government, and he for refusing to destroy his gods.
Next day the message was confirmed.   Kamehameha,
a remarkable man, had passed away.   On his death-bed
he asked an American trader to tell him about the Americans' God; but, said the native informant, in his broken
English, " He no tell him anything."   All the remaining
intelligence was also true.   The missionaries wrote in
their journal, " Sing, O heavens, for the Lord hath done
E

it." The brig soon anchored in Kailua Bay, the king's
residence ; and a fourteen days' consultation between the
king and chiefs followed. Certain foreigners opposed
their landing; " they had come to conquer the islands."
" Then," said the chiefs, " they would not have brought
their women." The decision was favorable. Messrs. Bingham, Loomis, Chamberlain, and Honoree go to Oahu ;
and Messrs. Ruggles and Whitney accompany the young
Tamoree to his father, the subject king of Kauai. The
meeting of father and son was deeply affecting. The old
king, for his son's sake, adopted Mr. Ruggles also as his
son, and·gave him a tract of land, with the power of a
chief. He prepared him a house, soon built a school-house
and chapel, and followed him with acts of friendship which
were of great benefit to the mission while the king lived,
and after his death. He himself became a hopeful convert, and in 1824 died in the faith.

When the missionaries were landed the brig sailed,
leaving them, out of three years' supplies provided by
the Board, one barrel of pork, one of beef, and one of
flour. But the kindness of the natives saved the mission
from want.

And now the missionaries settled down to their work.
They had found a nation sunk in ignorance, sensuality,
and vice, and nominally without a religion, though,
really, still in the grasp of many of their old superstitions. The old religion had been discarded chiefly on
account of its burdensomeness. We cannot here recount
all the agencies, outer and inner, which brought about
this remarkable convulsion. But no religious motives
seem to have had any special power. Indeed, King
Liholiho was intoxicated when he dealt to the system
its finishing stroke by compelling his wives to eat pork.

And by a providence as remarkable as inscrutable, the high priest threw his whole weight into the scale. Into this opening, thus signally furnished by the hand of God, the missionaries entered with wonder and gratitude. The natives educated in America proved less serviceable than was expected. Tenooe was soon excommunicated; although in later years he recovered, and lived and died a well-reputed Christian. Hopu and Honoree, while they continued faithful, had partly lost their native tongue, lacked the highest skill as interpreters, and naturally failed in judgment. Hopu, at the opening of the first revival, was found busy in arranging the inquirers on his right hand and his left hand, respectively, as they answered yes or no to the single question, " Do you love your enemies?" and was greatly disturbed at being interrupted.

The king and the chiefs, with their families, were the first pupils. They insisted on the privilege. Within three months the king could read the English language, and in six months several chiefs could both read and write. The missionaries devoted themselves vigorously to the work of reducing the native speech to writing; and in less than two years the first sheet of a native spelling-book was printed — followed by the second, however, only after the lapse of six months. From time to time several accessions of laborers were received from America, and various changes of location took place. The first baptized native was Keopuolani, the mother of the king; and others of the high chiefs were among the earlier converts. The leading personages, for the most part, showed much readiness to adopt the suggestions of the missionaries. In 1824 the principal chiefs formally agreed to recognize the Sabbath, and to adopt the ten commandments as the basis of government. They also soon passed a law forbidding females to visit the ships for immoral purposes.

The gravest obstacles encountered came from vile captains and crews of English and American vessels. They became ferocious towards the influences and the men that checked their lusts. The British whale-ships Daniel, and John Palmer, and the American armed schooner Dolphin, commanded by Lieutenant Percival, were prominent in open outrage. The house of missionary Richards was twice assailed by the ruffians of the ship Daniel, encouraged by their captain. On one occasion they came and demanded his influence to repeal the law against prostitution. On his refusal, they, in the presence of his feeble wife, threatened, with horrid oaths, to destroy his property, his house, his life, and the lives of all his family. Two days after, forty men returned, with a black flag, and armed with knives, repeating the demand. The chiefs at length called out a company of two hundred men, armed with muskets and spears, and drove them off. The crew of the Dolphin, with knives and clubs, on the Sabbath assailed a small religious assembly of chiefs, gathered at the house of one of their number, who was sick. Mr. Bingham, who was also present, fell into their hands, on his way to protect his house, and barely escaped with his life from the blow of a club and the thrust of a knife, being rescued by the natives. A mob of English and American whalemen, in October, 1826, started for the house of Mr. Richards, at Lahaina, with the intention of taking his life. Not finding him, they pillaged the town; while all the native women, from a population of four thousand, fled from their lust, for refuge in the mountains. A year later, the family of Mr. Richards took refuge in the cellar from the cannon-balls of the

John Palmer, which passed over the roof of the house.
When printed copies of the ten commandments were
about to be issued, this class of men carried their opposition, with threats, before the king. At Honolulu, while
the matter was pending, Mr. Ruggles was approached by
an American captain, bearing the satirical name of Meek,
who flourished his dagger, and angrily declared himself
ready " to bathe his hands in the heart's blood of every
missionary who had anything to do with it." At one
time, twenty-one sailors came up the hill, with clubs,
threatening to kill the missionaries unless they were
furnished with women. The natives, gathering for worship, immediately thronged around the house so thickly
that they were intimidated, and sneaked away. At
another time, fourteen of them surrounded the missionary, with the same demand, but were frightened off
by the resolute bearing of the noble chief Kapiolani — a
majestic woman, six feet high — who, arriving at the instant, swung her umbrella over her head, with the crisp
words, " Be off in a moment, or I will have every one
of you in irons." She was the same Christian heroine
who, in 1824, broke the terrible spell which hung over
the volcano Kilauea, by venturing down into the crater,
in defiance of the goddess Pele, hurling stones into the
boiling lake, and worshiping Jehovah on its black ledge.

It is easy to understand why a certain class of captains
and sailors have always pronounced the Sandwich Islands
mission a wretched failure.

The missionaries labored on undaunted. Eight years
from their landing found them at work, some thirty-two
in number, with four hundred and forty native teachers,
twelve thousand Sabbath hearers, and twenty-six thousand pupils in their schools. At this time, about fifty

natives, including Kaahumanu, the Queen Regent, and many of the principal chiefs, were members of the church. And now, in the year 1828, the dews of heaven began to fall visibly upon the mission. For two or three years the way had been preparing. Kaahumanu, converted in 1828, and several other high chiefs, had thrown themselves vigorously and heartily into the work. " They made repeated tours around all the principal islands," says Mr. Dibble, " assembling the people from village to village, and delivering addresses day after day, in which they prohibited immoral acts, enjoined the observance of the Sabbath, encouraged the people to learn to read, and exhorted them to turn to God, and to love and obey the Saviour of sinners." " The effect was electrical — pervading at once every island of the group, every obscure village and district, and operating with immense power on all grades and conditions of society. The chiefs gave orders to the people to erect houses of worship, to build school-houses, and to learn to read — they readily did so ; to listen to the instructions of the missionaries — they at once came in crowds for that purpose." About this time, too (May, 1825), the remains of King Liholiho and his wife were brought back from their unfortunate expedition to England, where they died from the measles. Their attending chiefs filled the ears of the people with what they saw in England ; and Lord Byron, commander of the British frigate which brought the remains, gave an honorable testimony to the missionaries.

These various influences caused a great rush to hear the Word of God. The people would come regularly, fifty or sixty miles, traveling the whole of Saturday, to attend Sabbath worship ; and would gather in little companies, from every point of the compass, like the tribes as they went up to Jerusalem. Meanwhile, the printed Word was circulated throughout the villages.

At length the early fruits appeared. In the year 1828, a gracious work began, simultaneously and without communication, in the islands of Hawaii, Oahu, and Maui. It came unexpectedly. The transactions at Kaawaloa (Hawaii) well illustrate the work. Mr. Ruggles was away from home, with Mr. Bishop, on an excursion to visit the schools of the island. They had been wrecked, and had swum ashore. Two natives, who were sent home for shoes and clothing, brought a message from Mrs. Ruggles to her husband, requesting his immediate return, for " strange things were happening — the natives were coming in companies, inquiring what they should do to be saved." He hastened back, and found the house surrounded from morning till night, and almost from night till morning. A company of ten or twenty would be received into the house, and another company would wait their turn at the gate. So it went on for weeks, and even months, and the missionaries could get no rest or refreshment, except as they called in Kapiolani and others of the converted chiefs to relieve them. Mr. and Mrs. Ruggles had the names of twenty-five hundred inquirers on their books. With multitudes, it was, no doubt, but sympathy or fashion; but there were also a large number of real inquirers, and many hopeful conversions. All the converts were kept in training classes a year before they were admitted to the church, and then only on the strictest examination. During the two following years, three hundred and fifty persons were received to communion at the several stations. For a time the work seemed to lull again, but in 1836 the whole aspect of the field was so inviting that the Board sent out a strong missionary re-enforcement of thirty-two persons, male and female.

At this time, and for the following year, the hearts of the missionaries were singularly drawn out in desires and prayers for the conversion, not only of the islands, but of America and of the world. And scarcely had the new laborers been assigned to their places, and learned the language, when (in 1838) there began, and continued for six years, one of the most remarkable awakenings that the world has ever witnessed. All hearts seemed tender. Whenever the Word was preached, conviction and conversions followed. The churches roused up to self-examination and prayer; the stupid listened; the vile and groveling learned to feel; the congregations became immense, and sometimes left their churches for the open air, and the prayer meetings left the lecture-room for the body of the church. There were congregations of four, five, and six thousand persons. The labors of the missionaries were almost incredible. They traveled through the islands, facing the storms and climbing the ravines, visiting, preaching, conversing, examining, in season, out of season. They preached from seven to twenty, or even thirty times a week; and the sense of guilt in the hearers often broke forth in groans and loud cries. Probably many indiscretions were committed, and there were many spurious conversions. But, after all allowances, time showed that a wonderful work was wrought. During the six years from 1838 to 1843, inclusive, twenty-seven thousand persons were admitted to the churches. In some instances the crowds to be baptized on a given Sabbath required extraordinary modes of baptism; and Mr. Coan, whose labors were incessant, and who baptized some seven thousand persons, is said to have sprinkled water with a brush upon the candidates as they came before him in throngs.

The next twenty years added more than twenty thousand other members to the churches, making the whole number received, up to the end of the connection with the American Board in 1863, some fifty thousand souls. Many of these had then been excommunicated — in some instances, it was thought, too hastily ; many thousand had gone home to heaven, and in 1863 some twenty thousand still survived in connection with the churches.

At length came the time when the islands were to be recognized as a nominally Christian nation, and the responsibility of their Christian institutions was to be rolled off upon themselves. In June, 1863, Dr. Anderson, Senior Secretary of the American Board, met with the Hawaiian Evangelical Association to discuss this important measure. After twenty-one days of debate, the result was reached with perfect unanimity, and the Association agreed to assume the responsibility hitherto sustained by the Board. This measure was consummated by the Board in the autumn following, and those stations no longer look to the American churches for management and control. " The mission has been, as such, disbanded and merged in the community."

On the 15th of January, 1864, at Queen's Hospital, Honolulu, died William Kanui (Tenooe), aged sixty-six years, the last of the native youth who gave rise to the mission and accompanied the first missionaries. He had wandered — had been excommunicated — and was restored ; and after many years of faithful service he died in the triumph of faith. In his last sickness he used " to recount the wonderful ways " in which God had led him. " The names of Cornelius, Mills, Beecher, Daggett, Pren-

tice, Griffin, and others were often on his lips; " and he
went, no doubt, to join them all above. God had spared
his life to see the whole miraculous change that had lifted
his nation from the depths of degradation to civilization
and Christianity. Could the spirit of Henry Obookiah
have stood in Honolulu, soon after the funeral of Kanui,
he would have hardly recognized his native island, except by its great natural landmarks. He would have
seen the city of Honolulu, once a place of grass huts and
filthy lanes, now marked by substantial houses and side-
walks, and a general air of civilization ; a race of once
naked savages decently attired, and living, some of them,
in comparative refinement ; a nation of readers, whom he
left without an alphabet ; Christian marriage firmly established in place of almost promiscuous concubinage ; property in the interior exposed with absolute security for an
indefinite time, where formerly nothing was safe for an
hour ; the islands dotted with a hundred capacious church
edifices, built by native hands, some of them made of
stone, most of them with bells ; a noble array of several
hundred common schools, two female seminaries, a Normal school for natives, a high-school that furnished the
first scholar to one of the classes in Williams College ; a
theological seminary and twenty-nine native preachers,
besides eighteen male and female missionaries sent to
the Marquesas Islands ; near twenty thousand living
church members ; a government with a settled constitution, a legislature, and courts of justice, and avowing the
Christian religion to be " the established national religion
of the Hawaiian Islands."

These facts exhibit the bright and marvelous aspect of
the case. But, of course, they have their drawbacks.
The Sandwich Islands are not Paradise, nor even Amer-

ica. The plane of civilization is, as it must be, far below that of our own country. The old habits still shade into the new. Peculiar temptations to intemperance and licentiousness come down by inheritance. Foreign interventions and oppositions have been, and still are, grave hindrances. Church members but fifty years removed from a state of brutalism cannot, and do not, show the stability, intelligence, and culture of those who inherit the Christian influences of a thousand years.

But the amazing transformation of the islands is a fact attested not alone by the statements of the missionaries, or of the Board that employed them. The most generous testimony has come from other sources. The Rev. F. S. Rising, of the American Church Missionary Society, explored the islands in 1866, for the express purpose of testing the question. He visited nearly every mission station, examined the institutions, religious, educational, social; made the personal acquaintance of the missionaries of all creeds, and conversed with persons of every profession and social grade. And he writes to the Secretary of the American Board, "The deeper I pushed my investigations, the stronger became my conviction, that what had been on your part necessarily an experimental work in modern missions had, under God, proved an eminent success. Every sunrise brought me new reasons for admiring the power of divine grace, which can lift the poor out of the dust, and set him among princes. Every sunsetting gave me fresh cause to bless the Lord for that infinite love which enables us to bring to our fellow-men such rich blessings as your missionaries have bestowed on the Hawaiian Islands. To me it seemed marvelous that in comparatively so few years, the social, political, and religious life of the nation should have undergone so

radical and blessed a change as it has. Looking at the
kingdom of Hawaii-nei, as it to-day has its recognized
place among the world's sovereignties, I cannot but see
in it one of the brightest trophies of the power of the
cross." " What of Hawaiian Christianity? I would
apply to it the same test by which we measure the
Christianity of our own and other lands. There are
certain outward signs which indicate that it has a high
place in the national respect, conscience, and affection.
Possessing these visible marks, we declare of any country
that it is Christian. The Hawaiian kingdom, for this
reason, is properly and truly called so. The constitution recognizes the Christian faith as the religion of the
nation. The Bible is found in almost every hut. Prayer
— social, family, and individual — is a popular habit.
The Lord's day is more sacredly observed than in New
York. Churches of stone or brick dot the valleys and
crown the hill-tops, and have been built by the voluntary
contributions of the natives. There the Word is preached,
and the sacraments administered. Sunday schools abound.
The contributions of the people for religious uses are very
generous, and there is a native ministry growing in numbers and influence, girded for carrying on the work so
well begun. The past history of the Hawaiian mission
abounds with bright examples, like Kaahumanu and
Kapiolani, and some were pointed out to me as I went
to and fro. They were at one time notoriously wicked.
Their lives are manifestly changed. They are striving
to be holy in their hearts and lives. They are fond of the
Bible, of the sanctuary, and prayer. Their theology may
be crude, but their faith in Christ is simple and tenacious.
And when we see some such in every congregation, we
know that the work has not been altogether in vain."

In 1860 Richard H. Dana, Esq., a distinguished Boston
lawyer, of the Episcopal Church, gave a similar testimony in the New York Tribune, during his visit to
the islands. Among other things, he mentions that
" the proportion of inhabitants who can read and write
is greater than in New England ; " that they may be seen
" going to school and public worship with more regularity
than the people at home ; " that after attending the examination of Oahu College, " he advised the young men
to remain there to the end of their course [then extending only to Junior year], as they could not pass the
Freshman and Sophomore years more profitably elsewhere, in my judgment ; " that " in no place in the world
that I have visited are the rules which control vice and
regulate amusement so strict, yet so reasonable, and so
fairly enforced ; " that " in the interior it is well known
that a man may travel alone with money through the
wildest spots unarmed ; " and that he " found no hut
without its Bible and hymn book in the native tongue,
and the practice of family prayer and grace before meat,
though it be no more than a calabash of poi and a few
dried fish, and whether at home or on a journey, is as
common as in New England a century ago."

There is one sad aspect about this interesting nation.
The population has been steadily declining since the
islands were first discovered. Cook, in 1773, estimated
the number of inhabitants at four hundred thousand.
This estimate, long thought to be exaggerated, is now
supposed to be not far from the truth. But in 1823, wars,
infanticide, foreign lust, imported drinks, and disease,
had reduced them to the estimated number of one hundred and forty-two thousand ; and in 1830, to the ascertained number of one hundred and thirty thousand. In

F

the lapse of a few years after the first visits of foreign
vessels, half the population are said to have been swept
away with diseases induced or heightened by their unholy
intercourse. The mission has done what could be done
to save the nation. But the wide taint of infamous diseases was descending down the national life before the
missionaries reached the islands ; and the flood-gates of
intemperance were wide open. The gospel has retarded
the nation's decline. But foreign influences have always
interfered — and now, perhaps, more than ever. The
sale of ardent spirits was once checked, but is now free.
The present monarch stands aloof from the policy of some
of his predecessors, and from the influence of our missionaries. And the population, reduced to sixty-two thousand in 1866, seems to be steadily declining. The Pacific Advertiser, which furnishes the facts, finds the
chief cause in the fearful prevalence, still, of vice and
crime, which are said to have been increasing of late ;
and the reason for this increase is "political degradation," and the readiness with which the people now obtain intoxicating drinks. It must be remembered that
" in the height of the whaling season, the number of
transient seamen in the port of Honolulu equals half the
population of the town ; " and the influences they bring
breathe largely of hell. Commercial forces and movements, meanwhile, are changing the islands. The lands
are already passing into the hands of foreign capitalists,
and the islands are falling into the thoroughfare of the
nations.

The proper sequel, therefore, of this grand missionary
triumph may be taken away ; and the race itself, as a
nation, may possibly cease to be. But in no event can
the value or the glory of the work achieved be destroyed

Not only will thousands on thousands of human souls thereby have been brought into the kingdom, by the labor of a hundred missionaries, and the expenditure of perhaps a million dollars from America, but a grand experiment will have been tried before the world, and an imperishable memorial erected for all time, of what the remedial power of the gospel can accomplish, in an incredibly short time, upon a most imbruted race. " Fifty years ago," says Dr. A. P. Peabody, " the half-reasoning elephant, or the tractable and troth-keeping dog, might have seemed the peer, or more, of the unreasoning and conscienceless Hawaiian. From that very race, from that very generation, with which the nobler brutes might have scorned to claim kindred, have been developed the peers of saints and angels." And all the more glorious is the movement, that the nation was sunk so low, and was so rapidly wasting away. " If the gospel," says Dr. Anderson, " took the people at the lowest point of social existence, — at death's door, when beyond the reach of all human remedies, with the causes of decline and destruction all in their most vigorous operation, — and has made them a Christian people, checked the tide of depopulation, and has raised the nation so on the scale of social life, as to have gained for it an acknowledged place among the nations of the earth, what more wonderful illustration can there be of its remedial power?"

The history of the Sandwich Islands will stand forever as the vindication to the caviler of the worth of Christian missions, and as a demonstration to the Christian of what they might be expected to accomplish in other lands, if prosecuted with a vigor at all proportioned to the nature and extent of the field, and crowned with the blessing of God.

The mission church must in due time turn missionary. So rightly reasoned the members of the Sandwich Islands mission. Thirty years had elapsed ; fifteen hundred dollars a year were collected at the monthly concert ; the first native pastor had been ordained by a council of native churches, and in the same year the members of the mission proposed that Hawaiian Christians should carry the gospel to other islands. The Prudential Committee at Boston warmly approved the proposal. Another year (1850) saw the Hawaiian Missionary Society formed at Honolulu.

Two thousand miles away to the south-west of Honolulu lie an immense number of islands — two thousand or more — now embraced under the general name of Micronesia — the Little Islands. Scattered in groups known by various appellations — Ladrones, Carolines, and the like — they stretch from three degrees south to twenty degrees north of the equator, and were then supposed to contain a population of two hundred thousand. Many of them were built wholly by the coral insect, and lie flat upon the water, while a few of them are basaltic islands, with mountains two or three thousand feet in height. These various groups differ in language and in the details of their customs and superstitions, but agree in the general characteristics of their native occupants. They are the natural homes of indolence and sensuality, of theft and violence. The warmth of the climate renders clothing a superfluity, and houses needless except for shade ; while the constant vegetation of the tropics dispenses with accumulated stores of food. A race of tawny savages stalk round almost or quite naked, swim like fish in the waters, or bask in the sunshine on shore. They prove as ready to catch, as vile sailors are to communicate, the vices of civilized lands. Intemperance is an easily besetting sin, and licentiousness is, with rare exceptions, the general and almost ineradicable pollution of the Pacific Islands. But in the Kingsmill group the missionaries found a people who, though practicing polygamy, held in honor the chastity of woman.

The attention of the missionaries was turned to three of these groups of islands — the Caroline, the Marshall, or Mulgrave, and the Kingsmill, or Gilbert Islands.

The eastern portion of the Caroline chain was naturally fixed upon as the centre of operations by reason of the convenient location and healthful climate. Two of these, Kusaie and Ponape, were the first to be occupied. Ponape, or Ascension Island, is a high basaltic island, sixty miles in circumference, surrounded by ten smaller basaltic islands, all inclosed within a coral reef. It rises to the height of two thousand eight hundred and fifty feet, and has its rivers and waterfalls. The island is a physical paradise, with a delightful climate, in which the range of the thermometer for three years was but seventeen degrees, and with a various and luxuriant vegetation. Among the indigenous products are the breadfruit, banana, cocoa-nut, taro, sugar-cane, ava, arrowroot, sassafras, sago, wild orange, and mango, with an immense variety of timber trees; while lemons, oranges, pine-apples, coffee, tamarinds, guava, tobacco, and other exotics thrive abundantly. From the mangrove trees that line the shore the ground rises by a series of natural terraces; and while twenty varieties of birds fill the air with life, a population of five thousand people are so hidden in the overhanging forests and shrubbery that but for an occasional canoe, or a smoke ascending, the passing vessel would scarcely know it to be inhabited. The inhabitants seem to be of Malay descent, and the place was " a moral Sodom."

Kusaie, or Strong's Island, the easternmost of the Carolines, is one of a small cluster, and is about thirty miles in circumference. It rises to the height of two thousand feet, wooded to the summit, and it then contained some one thousand five hundred people, strongly Asiatic both in look and speech. Here polygamy was unknown, and labor comparatively honorable. Many of the inhabitants, with an unusual quickness of apprehension, had learned of foreigners a kind of broken English before the missionaries arrived, and the Good King George, as his subjects called him, had, with surprising wisdom, forbidden the tapping of the cocoa-nut tree for the manufacture of intoxicating drink.

North-east of Kusaie lie the Marshall, sometimes called Mulgrave, Islands, subdivided into the Radack and Ralick, or eastern and western chains. About thirty principal islands compose the group. They are all of coral formation, but much higher, more fertile and inviting, than the Gilbert group, south of them. Majuro, or Arrowsmith, for example, is described as a magnificent island, rising eight or ten feet above the water at the landing-place, sprinkled with forests of breadfruit and pandanus trees, and abounding with cocoa-nuts and bananas. The population of the whole group was estimated at twelve thousand or upwards, speaking, to some extent, different languages. They had been comparatively uncontaminated by foreign intercourse from their reputation for ferocity. Several vessels had been cut off by them, and a great number of foreigners killed at different times, in retaliation for a former deadly attack upon the natives. The residence of the king and principal chiefs was at Ebon Island. The natives are in some respects superior to many of the Pacific islanders. Their features are sharper, their persons spare and athletic, and their countenances vivacious. The women wear their hair smoothly parted on the forehead, and neatly rolled up in the neck, sometimes adorned with flowers, and their skirts, fine and beautifully braided and bordered, extend from the waist to the feet. The men exhibit much more skill than is common in this region, and are fond of ornaments. Their comparative intelligence and exemption from foreign influence constituted the inviting aspect of this case; their alleged ferocity the formidable feature.

South-east from the Marshall Islands, on both sides of the equator, lie the Kingsmill, or Gilbert Islands. Fifteen or sixteen principal islands, surrounded by a multitude of islets, raised by the coral insect barely above the level of the ocean, contain a population of thirty or forty thousand, speaking mostly a common language resembling the Hawaiian. The land is densely covered with cocoa-nut groves. This is the "tree of a thousand uses," furnishing the natives almost "everything they eat, drink, wear, live in, or use in any way." Their hats, clothing, mats, and cords are made from its leaves; their houses are built from its timber; they eat the fruit, drink the milk, make molasses and rum from its juice, and manufacture from it immense quantities of oil for use and for sale. Their religion is the loosest system of spirit-worship, without priest, idol, or temple. They practice polygamy. The children go naked for ten or twelve years. The men wear a girdle, and the women a broader mat around them. Their appearance of nudity is relieved by the tattooing with which they are profusely and skillfully adorned. The considerable population, the unity of origin, faith, and language, and the general resemblance of their speech to the Hawaiian, rendered this group inviting, especially to the Sandwich Island laborers, although its torrid sun, comparatively barren soil, and limited range of vegetation made it not altogether favorable for the American missionaries' home.

Such was the region to which the gospel was to be carried. On the 18th of November, 1851, missionaries Snow and Gulick, with their wives, left Boston in the Esther May, and two months afterward, Mr. and Mrs. Sturges, in the Snow Squall, for Micronesia by way of the Sandwich Islands. Seven native Hawaiians were ready to join them, but two only, with their wives, were selected for the opening of the mission. The native churches made liberal contributions for their outfit and support. King Kamehameha III. gave them a noble letter of commendation to the Micronesian chiefs. A mission church was organized early in July, 1852, and on the 15th of the same month, just thirty-three years, or one whole generation, from the date of the former parting at Long Wharf, in Boston, the like scene took place in the harbor of Honolulu. A crowd of natives thronged the shore as the missionaries put off for the schooner Caroline. On the deck of the schooner there is a prayer in Hawaiian, and another in English, a verse of the Missionary Hymn, a shaking of friendly hands, and with a gentle breeze the vessel glides away.

The Caroline arrived at the Gilbert Islands, and on the 21st of August anchored at Kusaie. The missionaries were pleasantly received by Good King George in a faded flannel shirt, while his wife sat by in a short cotton gown, and his subjects approached him crouching on their hands and knees. He consented to the mission, gave them supplies, promised them land and a house, and on hearing the thirteenth chapter of Romans and witnessing their worship, he pronounced both to be " first rate." Messrs. Snow, Opunui, and their wives commenced their work in this isolated place, where at one time they passed a period of two full years without a letter from America. A fortnight later the Caroline anchored in the land-locked harbor of Ponape, where the king came on board, and after some conversation, told them it should be " good for them to stop." And here Messrs. Sturges, Gulick, Kaaikaula, and their wives were soon established in their new home.

In 1854 they were followed by Dr. Pierson and the native Hawaiian, Kanoa. These brethren brought a blessing to the crew of the whaling bark Belle that carried them ; her three mates were converted on the voyage. As they cruised among the Marshall Islands on their way to Kusaie, by a good providence, the king's sister, a remarkable woman, took passage from Ebon to another island, became attached to the missionaries, and spoke their praises at every island where they touched. The missionaries proceeded on their voyage to Kusaie, but with a deep conviction that the Lord was calling them back to the Marshall group.

At length (1857) the Morning Star, the children's vessel, heaves in sight at Kusaie. She brings Mr. and Mrs. Bingham, and Kanakaole, with his wife, on their way to the Marshall and Gilbert Islands. They are joined here by Messrs. Pierson and Doane, and sail for their destination. As they set out for Ebon Island, of the Marshall group, they are solemnly warned by old sea captains of the danger that awaits them from that

ferocious people. On approaching the island, the captain put up his boarding nettings, stationed his men fore
and aft, and anxiously awaited the issue. Fifteen canoes
drew near, jammed full of men. In the prow of the
foremost stood a powerful man with a wreath on his
head and huge rings in his ears. On they came, but in
the same instant Dr. Pierson and the savage recognized
each other as old acquaintances, and the savage came on
board shouting, " Docotor, docotor ! " in perfect delight.
Many months before, it seems, this man and a hundred
others had been driven by a storm upon Kusaie, where
the missionaries had rescued them, and befriended them
with food and medicine, and they had returned to their
homes in peace. So the Lord befriended the missionaries in turn, and prepared them a welcome among the
so-called cannibals. And when, after a further cruise
of thirty days, the Morning Star returned to leave the
missionaries at Ebon, they were met on the water by
twenty canoe loads of people shouting, singing, and
dancing for joy. On the shore they were received with
every demonstration of friendship, and the aged female
chief who had once sailed with Dr. Pierson among the
islands took him by both hands, and led him joyfully to
her house. On the same voyage Mr. Bingham and
Kanoa were set down at Apaiang, of the Gilbert group,
where the king gave them a pleasant home.

Thus was the gospel first carried to these three groups
of islands ; and here we leave them and their fellow-
laborers that followed them, chiefly Hawaiians, at their
self-denying toils. We will briefly sketch the progress
of the work on the principal island, Ponape, as a specimen of the whole. Here the king, though almost help-
less with the palsy, was friendly to the enterprise ; while

the Nanakin, his chief officer, expressed himself warmly, and received an English book with the avowed determination to learn to read it. "The cooper should teach him how, or he would pound him." Two short months sufficed to awaken the enmity of unprincipled foreigners. Two captains had bought one of the small islands, and made out a deed for the Nanakin to sign. He brought it to the missionaries, who found it to contain the grossest frauds, including even the forgery of the Nanakin's signature. The exposure, of course, created hostility. Six months brought fifteen vessels, and though in most instances the captains were friendly, and even kind, every arrival was attended with deplorable influences on the morals of the native women. Then came the opening of a school, some of the scholars sitting patiently for six long hours to get an opportunity to steal. Then came the small-pox, and before the end of the first year it had carried off multitudes of the inhabitants, broken up the school, arrested all plans of labor, prostrated the Hawaiian preacher, and produced a general recklessness and bitterness of feeling through the island. To add to the evil, the vaccine matter received from the Sandwich Islands proved worthless, and wicked foreigners circulated the report that the missionaries had introduced and were spreading the disease. By resorting boldly to inoculation, and beginning with the Nanakin, the missionaries at length saved many lives and regained confidence. In the midst of this calamity, Mr. Sturges' house burned up, with all its contents, driving him and his family to the woods. Hostilities arose, also, among the tribes, attended with robberies and murders, and the sailors continued to bring moral pollution. One day, in his accustomed tour, Mr. Sturges passed near three

brothels, all kept by foreigners. But the missionaries
toiled on, resumed their schools, gathered their growing
congregations, privately sowed the good seed, and in
four years' time were printing hymns and Old Testament
stories in Ponapean. After a night of eight years three
converts were at one time received to their little church.
followed by eight others soon ; and meanwhile a little
church of six members was formed in another part of the
island. Revivals brought opposition, and more or less
of persecution. At length a chapel was built in the
mountains by native hands, and at the principal station a
church edifice, forty feet by sixty, solemnly dedicated to
God. Hardly was it consecrated when the Morning
Star arrived with an eight hundred pound bell, the gift
of friends in Illinois ; and within a fortnight the Nanakin,
with his wife and fourteen other converts, sat down at
the table of the Lord. The chief had vibrated back and
forth — now proclaiming Sabbath observance, breaking
up five brothels, and following the missionary round the
island, and now distributing toddy profusely among the
people — till at length the Lord brought him in. Half
the islanders had by this time yielded an outward defer-
ence to the true religion. Early in the year 1867 there
were religious services regularly held at twelve principal
places, a thousand readers, one hundred and sixty-one
church members in good standing, and numbers of converts soon to be received. Three new churches had
been erected by the natives within two years, in one of
which (in May, 1867) one hundred communicants sat
down to the Lord's table, in the presence of six hundred
spectators, on the very spot where, fourteen years before,
Mr. Sturges was near being overcome and robbed ; and
another of these churches just built, though seating five

hundred persons, will soon need to be enlarged.   At
Kusaie there are one hundred and eighty-three church
members, of whom ninety-three were received in 1867.*
Three stone chapels had just been erected, four native
deacons ordained, and the eye of the missionary turned
to one man — the only living child of Good King George
— for a native pastor ; while the influence of the churches
is reacting on the sailors.   There are about sixty church
members now at the Marshall Islands, and the prospects
are eminently hopeful.   In the Gilbert group it is still
seed-time, but the knowledge is spreading from island to
island.

Among the laborers are ten Hawaiian missionaries,
who have toiled wisely and faithfully.   On many of these
islands the population is steadily growing less.   Possibly
the religious books that now exist in these several
tongues may one day lie, like Eliot's Indian Bible, without a reader ; but they will be monuments of noble
Christian self-denial, and mementoes of souls gathered
into the kingdom of heaven.

It remains to say a few words of the Marquesas.   The
mission here is in every aspect most remarkable, whether
we consider the character of the people, the origin, the
agency, or the influence of the mission.   The Marquesas
Islands, six in number, are situated nearly as far from
Micronesia as from Hawaii.   They are of volcanic formation, their mountains rising to the height of four or
five thousand feet, with a wonderful grandeur and variety
of scenery.   The climate is fine, and the valleys unsur-
passed in fertility, abounding in all manner of tropical
fruits and vegetation.   The fruits hang temptingly upon

* The statistics are of 1868.   See Appendix.

G

the trees, or drop on the ground. The islands contain
about eight thousand people, of Malay origin, speaking
a language very similar to the Hawaiian. The natives
have fine athletic forms, great vivacity and quick apprehension, but are to the last degree impatient of labor and
control. They are, in fact, among the most ,lawless,
quarrelsome, and ferocious of the tribes of men. They
have no acknowledged form of government. The individual gluts his revenge unhindered, and the clans in the
various valleys are in perpetual warfare. The bodies of
the slain are cut in pieces, and distributed among the
clan to be devoured, the little children even partaking
of the horrid meal. In 1859, when the whale-ship Star-
light was wrecked off the Island of Hivaoa, the natives
conspired to massacre the crew in order to plunder the
vessel, though in both objects they were frustrated. The
community cannot have forgotten the letter of President
Lincoln to the missionary Kekela, a few years ago,
thanking him for his services in rescuing the mate of an
American ship, Mr. Whalon, from being roasted and
eaten by these cannibals. The disposition of the natives
is to some degree symbolized by their personal appearance — the men hideously tattooed with lizards, snakes,
birds, and fishes, and the women smeared with cocoa-nut
oil and turmeric. Add to this the most oppressive system
of tabus, so that, for example, the father, the mother,
and the grown-up daughter must all eat apart from each
other, and we have some idea of the obstacles to the
Christian religion in those islands.

Some years ago a Hawaiian youth was left by a vessel
at these islands sick. He recovered, and by his superior
knowledge became a man of importance, and married
the daughter of the high chief Mattunui. The father-

in-law was so impressed with his acquisitions, which, as
he learned, were derived from the missionaries, that,
after consultation with the other chiefs, he embarked for
Lahaina to seek missionaries for Marquesas.   This was
in 1853.   The Hawaiian Society felt that the call was
from God.   Two native pastors — one of them Kekela —
and two native teachers, accompanied by their wives,
were deputed to go.   They were welcomed with joy.
Mattunui sat up all night to tell of the " strange things "
he saw and heard in the Hawaiian Islands; and an
audience of a hundred and fifty listened to preaching
on the following Sabbath.   The missionaries entered at
once on their various forms of Christian activity, organ-
izing their schools, and in due time translating the Gospel of John.   One foreigner alone was with them — Mr.
Bicknell, an English mechanic, a noble man, afterward
ordained a preacher ; otherwise the whole enterprise was
Hawaiian.   Roman Catholic priests hurried at once to
the islands, but the Hawaiian preachers held on, amid
immense discouragements, with great energy and perse-
verance, and with admirable good sense.   At length God
gave them the first convert, Abraham Natua.   Soon
after this the missionaries determined to break down the
system of tabus, and a great feast was gotten up on the
mission premises, at which the high chief Mattunui,
and many others, sat down for the first time with their
wives, and broke through the system in every available
direction.   It was a grand blow at the whole institution.
In four years the intolerable thievishness of the natives
was so far checked within the range of the missions that
clothing could be exposed, and the mission premises
could be left unlocked the entire day, with perfect safety.
Urgent calls came from various parts of the islands for

missionaries, five or six pieces of land — more than could be occupied — being given in Hivaoa alone. Converts came dropping in slowly, one by one, at first; and a quiet and powerful influence has been diffusing itself through the islands, and filling the minds of these devoted preachers with great hopes of the future. In 1867 there were eleven male and female missionaries at the islands, who had organized five churches with fifty-seven members, and were about to establish a boarding school for boys and another for girls. And in 1868 Mr. Coan, who had just visited the islands, wrote thus : "The light, and love, and gravitating power of the gospel are permeating the dead masses of the Marquesans. Scores already appear as true disciples of Jesus. Scores can read the Word of the living God, and it is a power within them. Hundreds have forsaken the tabus, and hundreds of others hold them lightly. Consistent missionaries and their teachings are respected. Their lives and persons are sacred where human life is no more regarded than that of a dog. They go secure where others dare not go. They leave houses, wives, and children without fear, and savages protect them. Everywhere we see evidence of the silent and sure progress of truth, and we rest assured that the time to favor the dark Marquesans has come." Whether we view the people on whom, or the people by whom, this power has been put forth, we see alike a signal movement of the gospel of Christ.

May, 1876.

Another edition of the foregoing sketch being called for, while using the stereotype plates as they stand, a few sentences will be added in regard to the Micronesia mission (still one of the missions of the American Board), bringing the statistics down to the present time. A reinforcement of American missionaries was sent to this field in 1874, consisting of Rev. Messrs. Horace J. Taylor and Robert W. Logan, and Mr. Frank E. Rand, a teacher, with their wives. The company sailed from Honolulu July 11, Mr. Taylor for Apaiang, the others for Ponape. Mrs. Taylor was removed by death in September, after having been but a few weeks in the field, leaving delightful evidence of her interest in, and hearty consecration to the work. Mr. and Mrs. Bingham were constrained to leave Apaiang in May, 1875, by the serious illness of Mr. Bingham, and they are now at the Sandwich Islands. The health of Mrs. Doane not permitting her to reside in Micronesia, Mr. Doane also felt that he must leave the field in 1875, and they are now connected with the Japan mission.

The progress of the work has been marked. Hawaiian missionaries now occupy six of the Gilbert and four of the Marshall Islands. Pingelap and Mokil, between Kusaie and Ponape in the Caroline Islands, have become out-stations, with Ponapean helpers and growing churches ; and more recently, in January, 1874, two islands of the Mortlock group, Lukunor and Satoan, about 300 miles southwest of Ponape, were occupied by three promising Ponapean laborers and their wives — three of the seven who were mentioned by Mr. Doane in June, 1873, as having been "licensed" for Christian work. They went to what was to them truly a *foreign* field, in the spirit, apparently, of full consecration, and have met with much encouragement. In October, 1875, Mr. Sturges and others visited these islands in the "Morning Star," and found such evidence that a considerable number of the people had already (after less than two years of labor

among them) heartily embraced the truth and become
true followers of Christ, that three churches were organized, with sixteen, fourteen, and eight members, respectively, and one of the Ponapeans was ordained as a pastor.

Mr. Doane, on leaving the field in 1874, made the following statements as to the progress of the work since the
" Caroline" took the first three mission families (Snow,
Gulick, and Sturges) to Micronesia, in 1852 : " These
first few laborers have been increased, till now there are
seven American missionaries, and eleven Hawaiians.
Four of the most important dialects of the field have been
reduced to writing, and into all of them the New Testament, or a portion of it, has been translated. More than
2,500,000 pages of school-books and of the Scriptures, have
been printed. More than 500 Christian songs have been
prepared, either original or translated. There are three
training schools, with 100 pupils, and many hundreds of
natives read well what has been printed for them. There
are about twenty churches, with a membership in the aggregate of about 1,200, giving, for each of the twenty-two
years of toil, forty-five conversions. The contributions at
the monthly concerts for the past year will be hard on to
$1,000, and not a small sum have the natives paid for books.
And from these churches there have been sent forth (and
partly supported by them) *ten catechists*, some as *home*,
some as *foreign* laborers ; and the so-called *foreign* ones
are emphatically so, going to a people of another dialect,
as foreign to them, almost, as to an American missionary."

MISSIONARIES, 1876.	Went Out.	Station.
Rev. Benjamin G. Snow	1851	Ebon.
Mrs. Lydia V. Snow	1851	
Rev. Albert A. Sturgis	1852	Ponape.
Mrs. Susan M. Sturgis	1852	
Rev. Hiram Bingham, Jr.	1856	Apaiang.
Mrs. Minerva C. Bingham	1856	
Rev. Joel F. Whitney	1871	Ebon.
Mrs. Louisa M. Whitney	1871	
Rev. Robert W. Logan	1874	Ponape.
Mrs. Mary E. Logan	1874	
Mr. Horace J. Taylor	1874	Apaiang.
Mr. Frank E. Rand	1874	Ponape.
Mrs. Carrie T. Rand	1874	

BARTLETT'S SKETCHES.

MISSIONS IN TURKEY.

IN a missionary point of view, Turkey is the key of Asia. Nowhere has the providential guidance of the missionary work been more remarkable. The divine hand has alike prepared the minds of the Armenian people in Turkey for Christian influences, directed attention thither, blessed the missionaries with wisdom, interposed continually for the protection of their work, and led them forward to a success already so broad and deep, as to be silently molding the destinies of the empire.

The first effort of the American Board in Asia Minor was quite wide of the mark. It was when, in 1826, Messrs. Gridley and Brewer were sent to Smyrna, the ancient home of Polycarp, to labor with the Greeks and Jews. The movement was attended with no great success, and the place became important chiefly as a printing station. The Mohammedans of the country meanwhile seemed inaccessible to all direct Christian labors.

But there was one most interesting people in the country, signally qualified to be the recipients and almoners of the divine grace. It is the old Armenian race, now widely scattered from their native Armenia, and dispersed everywhere in Turkey and Persia, and found even in India, Russia, and Poland. There are supposed to be at least three millions of them, more than half of whom are said

1

to be in Turkey. They are a noble race, and have been called " the Anglo-Saxons of the East." They are the active and enterprising class. Shrewd, industrious, and persevering, they are the bankers of Constantinople, the artisans of Turkey, and the merchants of Western and Central Asia. The nation received Christianity in the fourth century, and had a translation of the Scriptures made in the year 477 A. D., which is still extant and profoundly venerated, though now locked up, with many other religious works of theirs, in a dead language.

The Armenian church is a body as marked as the Roman Catholic or Greek church, strongly resembling them in deadness and formalism. Its head is the Catholicos. It holds to transubstantiation, invokes the saints, enforces confession and penance, teaches baptismal regeneration, priestly absolution, and the merit of good works, observes fourteen great feast days, one hundred and sixty-five fast days, and minor feasts more numerous than the days of the year. It has nine grades of clergy, some of whom are obliged to be once married, and performs all church services in the ancient Armenian, not one word of which is understood by the people. For purposes of persecution, as well as government, the Patriarch had, until recently, almost despotic power. But there are hopeful features even about this fossilized church. It openly adhered to the Christian name and profession under centuries of persecution and oppression. It regards the Word of God with almost unexampled reverence, so that when the Armenian is once convinced that any proposition is contained in the book he has learned to kiss at the altar, that is to him an end of all controversy. Another hopeful circumstance, directly connected with this, is that the errors of doctrine and practice with which the church is incrusted round, have never been fixed by any decree of council. Their standard of moral purity is also said to be immeasurably above that of the Turks around them, and they have a conscience which can be touched and roused. The enterprising character of the race, their wide dispersion, their preservation of the sentiment of national unity, and their acquaintance with the languages of the lands of their residence, render them a people of great promise for missionary purposes in those several lands.

A singular coincidence of judgment fixed the attention of the American Board upon this race. The missionary Parsons, on his first visit to Jerusalem, in 1821, encountered some Armenian pilgrims, whose interesting conversation drew from him the suggestion of a mission to Armenia itself. " We shall rejoice," said they, " and all will rejoice when they arrive." Mr. Fisk soon after wrote from Smyrna to Boston, recommending the measure. But before a word was heard from either, intelligent friends of the Board at home had urged the same proposal. At Beirut, Syria, among the earliest converts were the Armenian ecclesiastics (in 1826), two of whom, Bishop Dionysius and Krikor Vartabed, had traveled extensively in Asia Minor, and resided once in Constantinople. These brethren assured the missionaries that the minds of the Armenian people were wonderfully inclined towards the pure gospel, and that should preachers go among them, doubtless thousands of them would be ready to receive the truth. They themselves wrote letters to their countrymen, which excited no little attention.

During a dozen years or more, already, the British and Russian Bible Societies had put in circulation several thousand copies of the Scriptures in the ancient Armenian tongue, which were widely distributed in Turkey, and could be understood by the teachers and higher clergy; and at length they printed the New Testament in Armeno-Turkish and modern Armenian, intelligible to all who could read. Another important link in the chain of influences was the letter of Dr. King to the Roman Catholics, written on leaving Syria, and stating the reasons why he could not be a Papist. This letter, translated by Bishop Dionysius, and forwarded in manuscript to certain prominent Armenians in Constantinople, produced an extraordinary effect. A meeting was held, its Scripture references examined, and the determination adopted to do something to purify the church. One immediate effect was a training school for priests. At the head of it was placed Peshtimaljian, a profound scholar, a theologian, and a humble student of the Bible — a sort of oriental Melanchthon, even in his timidity. For while steadily exerting an evangelical influence, and silently guiding his pupils into new paths of inquiry, he was alarmed when he saw them joining the evangelical movement; and though at length he gained firmness enough to encourage their course, it was only on the year of his death that he openly declared his position. All the first converts at Constantinople were from his alumni.

In 1829 the Prudential Committee prepared the way, by the exploring tour of Messrs. Smith and Dwight among the Armenians; and two years later the noble Goodell began his work at Constantinople, to be followed in due time by the admirable band of associates, Dwight, Riggs, Schauffler, Schneider, Hamlin, Bliss, Powers, Pratt, Wheeler, and others, whose names are as household words in the churches. Their firmness, fidelity, and wisdom have been the theme of frequent commendation from foreigners in public as well as in private life.

The first missionaries, Goodell and Dwight, seemed compelled, by the circumstances of the case, to reach the people, at first, chiefly by means of schools and the press.

The several translations of the Bible, — Armenian, Armeno-Turkish, Osmanli-Turkish, Hebrew-Spanish, Hebrew-German, and finally Bulgarian, — and the various other books which they and their coadjutors have gradually sent forth, till they amount to a great body of literature, proved in due time to be the planting of siege guns, and the unlimbering of heavy artillery.

When Mr. Goodell called upon the Patriarch to seek his co-operation in establishing popular schools on an improved plan, that blandest of Orientals promised to send schoolmasters to learn the new method, and assured him of a love for the missionary and his country so profound, that if Mr. Goodell had not come to visit him, he must needs have gone to America to see Mr. Goodell! The one assurance meant as much as the other. The Patriarch promised again and again, but never moved till he moved in opposition. For nearly two years the missionaries gained little access to the Armenians. But God brought the Armenians to them.

The dawn of hope began in January, 1833, when young Hohannes Der Sahagyan came to open his heart. Some years before his father had bought a cheap copy of the New Testament, which the young man read and pondered, and compared with the principles and practices of his church. Then he joined the school of Peshtimaljian, where his inquiries were encouraged and aided. He was joined by his friend Senekarim, and for two years and a half they were seeking and praying together for light, unable to grasp the great and simple doctrine of salvation by grace alone. At length a hostile report turned their attention to the missionaries, and to them they went, first Hohannes, and afterwards both together, saying, " We are in a miserable condition, and we need your help. We are in the fire ; put forth your hands and pull us out." They soon found peace in believing, and became active laborers for the truth. From that point there appeared tokens of the constant presence of the Holy Spirit among the people. Opposition was speedily aroused, the school broken up, and for a time the press was stopped at Smyrna. But the good work went on. The number of attendants at Mr. Goodell's weekly meeting, and of visitors at the houses of the missionaries, steadily increased, and their errand was to talk of the way of salvation. The Bible was eagerly sought for, and the disposition to talk on religious subjects spread through the city, the suburbs, and the villages on the Bosphorus. In every circle there were found defenders of the truth, and occasionally a sincere believer. An influence was abroad which Mr. Goodell characterized as a " simple and entire yielding of the heart and life to the sole direction of God's Word and Spirit." Evangelical sermons began to be heard from the priests.

The missionary force was increased. A high school was opened at Pera, and stations occupied at Broosa and Trebizond. A school for girls — a novel thing in Turkey — was opened at Smyrna. The missionaries steadily pursued the policy of disseminating the truth, without making attacks upon the Armenian church. Still, opposition was more and more aroused, but was either frustrated or overruled to the furtherance of the mission. Then the wealthy bankers of Constantinople determined to crush the high school. To provide a substitute, they founded a college in Scutari, and remodeled the national school in the quarter of Hass Keuy, which they committed to the supervision of a great banker residing there. In breaking up the high school, the vicar who conveyed the message unwittingly informed the boys for the first time that the sign of the cross is not enjoined in the Scriptures. And when Hohannes Sahagyan was suddenly removed from his school of forty, to the amazement of all concerned, he was engaged by the banker of Hass Keuy to take charge of that school of *six hundred*. Every effort was made to shake the banker's decision, but though he had never been known as favoring the evangelical cause, he was perfectly firm ; and so Sahagyan was advanced to a post of far greater influence and freedom, which he held for two years with marked success.

The year 1839 witnessed a deep-laid plot for the expulsion of Protestantism from the land, suddenly overthrown by the providence of God. The enemies of the mission had enlisted some of the Sultan's chief officers, and even gained the ear of the Sultan himself. Sahagyan and two other persons, a teacher and a converted priest, were arrested, imprisoned, and, with much personal cruelty, banished. The mild Armenian Patriarch was deposed, and his place filled by a man of violence ; bulls were issued by both the Greek and Armenian Patriarchs, prohibiting the reading or possession of all missionary books, and even all intercourse with the missionaries. Long lists of heretics were made out, and the storm seemed about to descend in its fury, when the hand of the persecutors was arrested by the hand of God. The rebellious Pacha of Egypt was the instrument of rescue. The Sultan, with his broken army, was suddenly forced

8   SKETCHES OF THE MISSIONS.

to call on the Patriarchs for several thousand recruits. Then came the utter defeat of his army, the death of the sultan before he heard the tidings, the surrender of the whole Turkish fleet, the succession of the boy Abdqol Medjid to the throne, and the threatened dissolution of the Turkish empire. The persecution was effectually stayed. By a remarkable providence, the young Sultan, unsolicited by his people, granted them a charter of civil protection and religious liberty.

The commotions concerning the missionaries gave them publicity, and brought inquirers. In 1840 Messrs. Dwight and Hamlin visited Nicomedia, where, two years before, Mr. Dwight had found a little company of believers who had been led to the truth by a copy of the Dairyman's Daughter, and other printed tracts. While here a merchant from Adabazar was induced, by the warning letter of the patriarch, to come and visit them. The report and the tracts with which he returned to Adabazar were the beginning of a good work; and when, in the following year, Mr. Schneider, in response to repeated invitations, visited the place, he found there already a little band of converted men. In 1843 a young Armenian, who had embraced and renounced Mohammedanism, was publicly beheaded in the streets of Constantinople. But this event became the occasion on which the English ambassador, supported by the ministers of France, Prussia, and Austria, extorted from the sultan a written pledge that no person thenceforward should be persecuted for his religious opinions. The British ambassador declared the transaction to be little less than a miracle. And though the pledge has been often evaded and violated in practice, it stands as a great landmark in the religious history of the empire. The Patriarch himself, two years later, made a fixed attempt to violate this guaranty, which redounded speedily to the establishment of the faith. He issued a sentence of excommunication against all adherents of the new doctrines, which was accompanied by scenes of shocking violence in the chief cities of the empire. Christians were stoned in the streets, unjustly imprisoned, ejected from their shops, invaded and plundered in their houses, bastinadoed, and abandoned by their friends. It marked an era in their history. For after meekly and nobly enduring this protracted abuse, they were, by the resolute efforts of the foreign ambassadors, headed by Sir Stratford Canning, taken forever from under the patriarch's jurisdiction, and organized into a separate Protestant community. On the 1st of July, 1846, was formed at Constantinople the first Evangelical Armenian church in Turkey, with a native pastor; and during that summer similar churches were formed in Nicomedia, Adabazar, and Trebizond.

The enemy had overdone his work. The excommunication was a blunder; for it founded four Protestant churches the first year. And the previous measures had been equally blundering. For, remarkable as was the spirit of inquiry among the Armenians, it had been vastly increased by the measures taken to put it down. The enemies of a pure gospel had done an immense amount of gratuitous advertising almost from the first. The Romish Patriarch had (in 1836) tried his hand at a public denunciation of the missionaries and their books. Four years later, the Armenian Patriarch had issued a " bull," followed in a fortnight by a bull from the Greek Patriarch, both of the same description, and by an imperial firman apparently re-enforcing them, and in another six weeks by still another Armenian

H

bull, with terrific anathemas. A Patriarchal letter had been sent to Trebizond in 1840; and in January, 1846, two successive and still more furious anathemas had been issued by the Patriarch in his official character, with the lights extinguished, and a vail before the altar, whereby the adherents of the new gospel were "accursed, excommunicated, and anathematized by God, and by all his saints, and by us." They were printed, and sent to all the churches. For six months continuously was this anathema kept dinning every Sabbath in the ears of the faithful, till cursing grew stale. The final excision that year (July) was read in all the Armenian churches.

So much thundering sent many flashes of light through the dark. The Patriarch had better facilities for advertising than the missionaries. He unquestionably sent them a multitude of inquirers. Thus his letter of warning brought the merchant of Adabazar to Messrs. Dwight and Hamlin at Nicomedia for information; and he it was who carried back the Testament and tracts that began the good work there. Many an inquirer came to ascertain personally of the missionaries whether the stories were true that the Americans were a nation of infidels, without church or worship.

When the Patriarch had hurried Bedros, the vartabed, out of the city for his Protestant tendencies, the vartabed had gone distributing books and preaching throughout the whole region of Aleppo and Aintab. When he had sent priest Vartanes a prisoner to the monastery of Marash, and then banished him to Cesarea, Vartanes had first awakened the monks, and then preached the gospel all the way to Cesarea.

The missionaries wisely availed themselves of this

rising interest, in tours for preaching, conversing, and distributing religious treatises. Messrs. Powers, Johnston, Van Lennep, Smith, Peabody, Schneider, Goodell, Everett, Benjamin, pushed forth to Aintab, Aleppo, Broosa, Harpoot, Sivas, Diarbekir, Arabkir, Cesarea, and various other places, through the empire.

They soon found that they were in the midst of one of the most extraordinary religious movements of modern times, silent, and sometimes untraceable, but potent and pervasive. In every important town of the empire, where there were Armenians, there were found to be, as early as 1849, one or more " lovers of evangelical truth." But it was no causeless movement. The quiet working of the " little leaven " was traceable almost from its source by indubitable signs. It was a notable sight to see, when, in 1838, the vartabed and leading men of Orta Keuy, on the Bosphorus, where the missionaries first gained access to the Armenians, went and removed the pictures from the village church. It was a notable thing to hear, when, in 1841, the Armenian preachers of Constantinople were discoursing on repentance and the mediatorial office of Christ. It was another landmark, when, in 1842, the fervor of the converts not only filled the city with rumors of the new doctrines, but, after a season of special prayer, held in a neighboring valley, sent forth Priest Vartanes on a missionary tour into the heart of Asia Minor. A still more significant fact it was, when, in that year and the next, the Armenian women were effectually reached and roused, till family worship began in many a household, and a Female Seminary at Pera became (in 1845) a necessity. The brethren had observed the constant increase of inquirers, often from a distance, and they had found, even in 1843, such

a demand for their books as the press at Smyrna was
unable fully to supply.   In many places, as at Nicomedia,
Adabazar, and Aintab, books and tracts began the work.

The preaching services at Constantinople would be
occasionally attended by individuals from four or five
other towns, and at Erzroom one Sabbath (February,
1846) there were attendants from six different places.
The Seminary for young men at Bebek (a suburb of
Constantinople) drew visitors from great distances, and
from all quarters, as far as Alexandria, St. Petersburg,
and the Euphrates.   The native brethren also had been
engaged in disseminating the truth, and the first awakenings at Killis, Kessab, and Rodosto, for example, were
due to their labors.   And thus, though the movement
rolled on at last with great power and speed, the prep-
aration had been long and broad.   Yet not without
abundant and fierce opposition.   Indeed, the resistance
was so common, sooner or later, that it gives only a
glimpse at the facts, to tell how, even at Constantinople,
the brethren and one of the missionaries were once pelted
with stones; how the little band at Nicomedia were at
times compelled to hold their worship, somewhat like
the early Christians and the Covenanters, in distant
fields, and even after religious liberty was proclaimed,
were abused in the streets, and had their houses stoned;
how, at Adabazar, a Protestant teacher was put in chains
and in prison; how at Trebizond the very women at-
tacked with stones two of their own sex, as they returned
from the preaching, and the husbands who protected
their own wives were thrown into prison and the stocks,
like Paul and Silas of old; how the mob at Erzroom
burst into the house of Dr. Smith, and destroyed his
books and furniture; and how, in 1847, Mr. Johnston

was expelled from Aintab by the governor, and stoned out
of town by Armenian school-boys and teachers, although
the very next year Aintab became the seat of a church
that grew with singular rapidity, and a great centre of
Christian activity. These things died out only by degrees; not until after the Sultan had issued his firmans,
first (in 1850) placing the Protestants on the same basis
with other Christian communities; and again (in 1853)
placing his Christian subjects on the same level with
Mohammedans before the law; and yet once more (in
1856) granting full "freedom of conscience and of religious profession.;" not until long after three Patriarchs,
Stepan, Hagopos, and Matteos, had tried each to outdo
his predecessor in severity, and the third of them had
(in 1848) been deposed for financial frauds.

It was in the year 1849 that the missionaries, with
five native pastors ordained already, and with the clear
recognition of the broad fields now white for the harvest,
adopted a Report, setting forth to the native Christians
the great duty of supporting their pastors and religious
institutions, relieving the missionaries for other fields,
and themselves engaging " in the further extension of the
truth." Next year they turned and asked the home
churches for twelve more missionaries, to oversee this
wonderful uprising. For several years in succession the
Board repeated the call for " twelve more missionaries."
For two years six only answered. " From every part of
the land," wrote Mr. Dwight, in 1853, " there comes to
us one appeal, ' Send us preachers, send us preachers ; ' "
and Mr. Schneider wrote home, " I almost fear to have
the post arrive." Six other laborers responded in 1854;
and next year came the urgent call for " seventeen," to
meet the great emergency.

The Crimean war for three or four years agitated the nation and the nations. But the spiritual reformation rolled on ; it was a mightier and a deeper force. It was impossible for the missionaries to keep pace with the calls. The wonder is, that they could accomplish so much as they did. At one time (1855) they hurried five young students into the ministry before their studies were completed. But they felt and wrote that they were losing opportunities all the time. And they were right. Humanly speaking, it seemed as though with a sufficient missionary force the Armenian element of Turkey could have been carried everywhere by storm.

From this time forth the enterprise became too broad even to trace in this rapid way. If the whole movement shall ever be suitably recorded, the history of *this* reformation will be second in interest to no other that ever has been written. There are scores and scores of villages, each of which would furnish materials for a volume ; and multitudes of cases that recall the fervor, faith, and fortitude of apostolic times. Let us hope that they may find their adequate historian. For the present we can only refer to the contemporary pages of the Missionary Herald.

The breadth of the movement began also to demand new missionary centres. The book depository, which had been on the north side of the Golden Horn, planted itself boldly (1855) in the heart of Constantinople ; and six or eight boxes of books might be seen at a time, marked to "Diarbekir," "Arabkir," "Cesarea," "Aintab," and so on. The Seminary proved inadequate to the demand for preachers and teachers, and the organization of other seminaries about this time at Tokat and Aintab, indicated the time as not distant when there should be three missions, instead of one, in Asiatic Turkey. Indeed, Mr. Dunmore was writing, in 1857, that "forty men" were needed at once, as teachers and preachers around Harpoot; and Dr. Hamlin was urgently pressing the wants of the Bulgarians in European Turkey.

One of the most delightful instances of Christian magnanimity was displayed in England about this time. The financial troubles of 1857 in America had embarrassed the Board, and threatened serious embarrassment to this mission. Noble Christians in England, of all Evangelical communions, including ministers of the Church of England, came at once to the rescue. They formed the " Turkish Missions Aid Society," invited Dr. Dwight to present our cause in England, and raised money thenceforward, not to found missions of their own in Turkey, but to aid ours. At an anniversary of the Society in 1860, the Earl of Shaftesbury crowned this magnanimity of deeds by an equal magnanimity of words. He said of our missionaries in Turkey, " I do not believe that in the whole history of missions, I do not believe that in the history of diplomacy, or in the history of any negotiation carried on between man and man, we can find anything to equal the wisdom, the soundness, and the pure Evangelical truth of the men who constitute the American mission. I have said it twenty times before, and I will say it again, — for the expression appropriately conveys my meaning, — that they are a marvelous combination of common sense and piety."

At this point, the enterprise, like a Banyan tree, changed its branches into new roots, and henceforth was reported as the Western, Central, and Eastern Turkey missions. The main feature of interest became that of sure but gradual growth.

The Western Turkey mission-field covers a region of singular historic interest. It includes alike the field of Troy and of the "Seven Churches." It probably saw the origin both of the Iliad and the Odyssey, and of the Apocalypse and the fourth Gospel. In its north-western portion flows the little river Granicus, where Alexander first defeated the Persian armies, and in its south-western part lies the once world-renowned seaport of Miletus, where Paul made his affecting speech to the elders who had come from Ephesus, that seat of the marvelous temple of Diana, and of the church of the "Ephesians." The poor little village of Isnik, too small for a mission station, is all that remains of the Nicæa, famous for the Nicene Creed, framed in a council where Constantine presided — a city long the bulwark of Constantinople against the Turks, then the capital of the Sultan Solyman, and afterwards retaken by the first crusaders. The centre of missionary operations is the great city of unparalleled site and matchless harbor, rebuilt by Constantine, the object of six captures, and more than twenty sieges, the ignis fatuus that turned the first Napoleon towards Moscow rather than St. Petersburg, the long-coveted treasure of the Russian czars, and the place of five great Christian councils. Broosa, another of our stations, is at the ancient capital of the Ottoman empire; and its castle is said to commemorate the time and the work of Hannibal the Carthaginian. Nicomedia, still another station, was once the capital of the Bithynian kings, the home of Diocletian when he ruled the Eastern empire, and the place where poison ended the life of Hannibal. One of the stations last occupied, Manissa, is the old Magnesia, where the two Scipios defeated Antiochus the Great, and won for Rome the empire of the East.

In this region, covered thick with historic associations, the twenty-four churches, with their thousand members, their twenty-nine pastors and licensed preachers, and their forty-five hundred enrolled Protestants, only indicate the deep under-current of influence now at work. A considerable body of missionaries are still furnishing the original forces. The press pours forth some fifty thousand volumes and thirty thousand tracts a year, in six different languages, including the English. Two "Evangelical Unions" of native churches and pastors have been formed, and the churches contribute already to Christian objects four thousand dollars a year. A theological seminary, and a ladies' boarding-school, now at Marsovan ; two other girls' schools ; training classes at Broosa and Sivas ; Robert College, the indirect child of the mission, now looking out conspicuously over the Bosphorus, with its hundred and eighty students of seventeen different nationalities ; and last, not least, a band of lady missionaries finding their way into the homes and hearts of their sisters, — these are some of the influences unfalteringly at work in the heart of the Turkish empire.

The Central Turkey mission numbers among its thirty stations and out-stations Antioch, the old " Queen of the East," long the chief city of Asia, if not of the world, then the residence of Syrian kings, and afterwards of Roman governors, the place where "the disciples were first called Christians;" Aleppo, which succeeded Palmyra in the trade between Europe and the East, still the commercial centre of Northern Syria ; Oorfa, a traditional " Ur of the Chaldees ; " and Tarsus, where Paul was born, and Alexander nearly died. Here twenty-two churches comprise eighteen hundred members, and average congregations of more than five thousand persons.

with eight thousand registered Protestants. A theological seminary, with thirty-seven students, at Marash; two female seminaries; eighteen hundred and forty communicants in twenty-two churches, some of which carry all their own expenses, while the whole body contribute six thousand dollars in gold for Christian charities; eight thousand registered Protestants; nineteen pastors and preachers; an Evangelical Union, courageous enough to plan a Christian college, and to gain pledges from their own churches of nine thousand dollars for the purpose; a strong staff of lady missionaries working most hopefully among their sex; and a general diffusion of light among both Armenians and Mohammedans, which no figures can display, — indicate a hold of the gospel in this region so strong as to raise the question of " closing up the proper missionary work in Central Turkey at no distant day." An amount and variety of active Christian effort has been put forth here, and a long-continued religious agitation awakened from such centres as Aintab and Marash, which no one can understand, except as he traces back the letters of the missionaries for the last fifteen years. The history of all the commotions at Aintab, from the time when Mr. Johnston was stoned out of town to the time when it has become the seat of two self-supporting churches, with native pastors and near five hundred members, surrounded by a cluster of thirteen out-stations, containing nearly four hundred more church members, would require a volume. The whole course and working of the mission are far too remarkable to be dismissed in this summary way. There is a wide-spread expectation of a coming change, of which the two hundred and twenty members admitted to the churches during the last year are but the few drops before the shower.

The Eastern Turkey mission deserves special mention for the method and rapidity of its achievements. Coming later, for the most part, than the other divisions of the Turkish missions, it was enabled to build on their foundation and profit by their experience. Its methods have been largely the same which were employed in Turkey from the beginning, and specially and powerfully developed in the central mission, but perhaps still more concentrated here. We have also the advantage of a very full narration from the chief actors in the scene. Their vigorous and invigorating work, novel not so much in conception as in execution, bids fair to mark an epoch in the history of missions. The territory includes, at Mosul, the site of Nineveh, and in ancient Armenia, probably the cradle of the human race. The gospel is carried to the region of "the Fall." One portion of this territory, the Harpoot mission field, has been the scene of a most interesting and remarkable experiment. About fourteen years ago, Messrs. Wheeler and Allen, with their wives, entered on this field, followed, after two years, by Mr. H. N. Barnum and his wife. The region committed to them was somewhat larger than Massachusetts, containing twenty-five hundred villages, and a population of five hundred thousand persons. These brethren went with the determination to introduce a self-supporting, self-propagating religion; to offer Christianity " as a leaven," and not as a " leavened loaf;" to confer privileges which in the reception should test the self-denial of the recipient. They adhered to three fundamental, and, as they thought, apostolical principles: First, to " ordain elders in every church," giving a pastor from among the people to every church at its formation; Second, to leave each church to choose its own pastor, make its own pecuniary engagements with him, and assume the responsibility of fulfilment. Temporary aid might be granted, to the amount of one half the salary, to be reduced each year, and in five years to cease. The third principle was to make the churches at once independent of missionary control.

These points were not carried without a hard struggle, and often bitter opposition. It took seven years to bring the church at Harpoot up to the entire support of its pastor. All their firmness, patience, ingenuity, and energy were taxed to the utmost; but they carried it, and the next three were made self-supporting more easily than that one. They determined in like manner to do for the people in all respects only just what would enable them to do for themselves. They put upon them nearly the whole cost of their church edifices. In their schools they taught no English, to tempt their young men into foreign employments. They insisted that their converts, even those who pointed to their gray hair in remonstrance, should learn to read the Bible, and that those who had learned should go and teach others, especially their wives. After the schools were fairly under way they threw the support of them upon the natives. Their books, the Scriptures included, they made it a rule to sell at some price, but never to give away. Almost without exception those who bought books were first taught to read them; and the main dependence has been on the Bible — read, preached, and sung. The sacred volume itself, without the living preacher, has, in frequent instances, borne blessed fruit. Thus, in the village of Bizmishen, "thief" Maghak bought a Bible, learned to read it, became an honest man and Christian, and established public worship with a good chapel and the nucleus of a little church in his village. Another Bible, sold by him, gathered an audience of thirty men and women at Najaran, forty miles away, to hear the Bible read and explained. In another instance, a colporteur, spending the night at Perchenj, found seventy men assembled in a stable, listening to one who was reading the Bible. Messrs. Wheeler and Barnum visited the place, spent a Sabbath, and sent them a teacher. A revival followed, and in two years the little church numbered forty members, with twenty-one hopeful converts, and a native pastor settled over them, and owned a chapel and a parsonage. These brethren, self-moved, organized a missionary society to go, two and two, into the neighboring villages, to explain and sell the Bible. Two of them entered Hooeli, a village where the missionaries had repeatedly and vainly endeavored to gain a foothold. They prayed as they went, "O Lord, give us open doors and hearts." Their prayer was answered. The villagers applied to the missionaries for a teacher; but as none could be had, the men of Perchenj sent one of their own number to begin the work. Soon after, a seminary student went to spend his summer vacation there, and a mob pitched him and his effects into the street. But the leaven was working. A place of worship, holding three hundred persons, was erected; schools were opened to learn the Bible; a blessed awakening came, attended with forty or fifty conversions, including some of the most hopeless cases in the village; and at the last information they were about to organize a church, and to settle and support as pastor one of the men who first came with the Bible and a prayer to God for a hearing.

Such is the nature of the work. Every church and every community of Bible readers has a Bible society,

I

that sends forth its books in bags on the backs of donkeys; and the churches send forth their members, two by two. for days and weeks together, in the home missionary work. The community of Harpoot had thirty-five members thus engaged at one time. They are also prosecuting a " Foreign Missionary " enterprise in a region extending from four to twenty days' journey to the south. This movement is aided by the theological students in their long vacation — the seminary being founded on the principle of accustoming students to pastoral work while pursuing their studies. These young men are trained to be Bible men and practical men. When on one occasion they were found to be above doing some necessary manual labor at the seminary, they were brought to their senses by a reduction of their beneficiary aid.

The persevering and often amusing methods by which a penurious people have been made generous and self-sacrificing, and the modes in which the missionaries have persisted in doing the work, not of mere educators, nor even of pastors, but of Christian missionaries, infusing the " leaven," must be learned from Mr. Wheeler's book, " Ten Years on the Euphrates." It is as brimful of instruction for the home field as the foreign. Would that many of the home churches might be brought up to the same level.

So thoroughly has the spirit of independent action been infused into these churches, that, in 1865, they organized themselves into an " Evangelical Union," with a thorough system of Christian activity, Bible distribution, Education Society, Home and Foreign Missions, and church erection. The fruits are yet largely in the future — we may hope, in the near future. The missionaries are already feeling that the time is not distant when they can leave this field for another. Already is their work represented by eighteen churches, — ten of them entirely independent, — by seventy out-stations, by a hundred and twelve native preachers, pastors, and other helpers, " by thousands of men and women reading the word of God, and by thousands more of children and youth gathered into schools; in a word, by the foundations of a Christian civilization laid upon a sure basis in the affections of an earnest, self-sacrificing, Christian community."

Many outward tokens begin to show the silent power of this mission. In Harpoot city and its seventy out-stations, in which years ago were two hundred and fifty-six priests, there were in 1867 but one hundred and forty-five. The revenue of the monasteries is passing away. The monastery of Hukalegh, which once collected three hundred measures of wheat from that village and Bizmishen, then collected but eighteen. The cause of temperance is advanced; believers spontaneously leave off wine-drinking. A wonderful elevation has taken place in the character and position of woman. " How happens it," said a man one day to Mr. Wheeler, " that *all* the missionaries' wives are angels? " But now, says Mr. Wheeler, " some of them there have angels too for their companions." One of the most blessed fruits of the gospel is seen in its effects on the family circle. These believers " are as careful to maintain secret, family, and social prayer as Christians in this land, and the last more so." The Sabbath is carefully and conscientiously kept by them. And in their Christian liberality they seem to be an example to the best churches of this country.

The Eastern Turkey mission, of which Harpoot is a principal station, now occupies one hundred and six out-stations, and has twenty-eight churches, containing a

thousand members, with average congregations of fifty-
five hundred persons.   Nearly, if not quite, half the
churches are self-supporting.   Twenty-seven native pastors and twenty-three licensed preachers are dispensing
the gospel, and sixty-two young men are now training
for the ministry.   The Evangelical Union is maintain-
ing four missionary stations among the mountains of
Koordistan.

In glancing over the present religious aspect of Asiatic
Turkey, it is impossible not to feel that the seeds of great
events have been widely sown.   Seventy-four churches,
with four thousand members, an average attendance of
fourteen thousand persons, and about twenty thousand
registered Protestants ; a hundred native preachers, occupying more than twice that number of places, scattered
through the empire, who have received five hundred
members in the year just passed ; a hundred and forty-
three young men on their way to the ministry ; four
Evangelical Unions, apparently able to carry on the
Lord's work, were every missionary taken away by the
providence of God ; a Christian press, pouring forth
ten million pages in a year ; a general spirit of inquiry
through the empire ; — all are tokens of changes, if not
of revolutions, in Turkey, which even this generation may
look upon with wonder.   He that is wise will watch the
course of events.

It is several years since Layard, the English explorer,
could testify that there was scarcely a town of importance
in Turkey without a Protestant community.   And now
we have a remarkable voice from within.   Hagop Effen-
di, the civil head of the Protestant community, has recently made a tour of observation through the empire, at the
charge of the sultan.   In his report he declares that

" those who have become Protestant in principle far exceed in number the registered Protestants, and those who are willing to avow themselves such. The indirect influence of Protestantism has been greater and healthier than what is apparent. The fact that eighty-five per cent. of the adults in the [Protestant] community can read, speaks greatly in favor of its members. Any one acquainted with the social condition and religious ideas of the Oriental people, who will take pains to compare them with the liberal institutions introduced, can readily imagine the state of society which must necessarily follow such a change. I should hardly do justice were I to pass without noticing the strictly sober habits of our people. The use of strong drink is very seldom found and habitual drunkenness is very rarely known. I was gratified to find everywhere a great improvement in domestic relations as compared with the condition of families before they became Protestants. I need not weary our friends with details to show the effect of the healthy influence of the various Protestant institutions — such as Sabbath schools, social prayer-meetings, women's meetings, and the little philanthropic associations coming into existence with the advance of Protestantism. The noble institutions and liberal organizations which have been introduced among this people are yet in their infancy ; and their power of elevating the individual man, in his moral and intellectual capacities, is not so apparent in the unsettled state of affairs which of necessity follows such a mighty social and religious revolution ; but they are objects of great interest and a source of great encouragement to every close observer of the course of affairs, even in the very confusion which is produced by them."

In a recent letter to Secretary Clark, he makes the following interesting statements : —

" *The most zealous advocate of American civilization could not have done half as much for his country abroad as the missionary has done.* The religious and social organizations, the various institutions introduced, are doing a great deal in introducing American civilization. From the wild mountains of Gaour Dagh, in Cilicia, you may go across to the no less wild mountains of Bhotan, on the borders of Persia ; or you may take Antioch if you please, and go on any line to the black shores of the Euxine ; you will certainly agree with me in declaring that the American missionary has served his country no less than his Master. Even in wild Kurdistan you will find some one who can reason with you quite in Yankee style, can make you a speech which you cannot but own to be substantially Yankee, with Yankee idioms and American examples to support his arguments ; and if you want to satisfy your curiosity still more, you may pay your visit to the schools established by the missionaries in the wild mountains of the Turkomans, in Kurdistan, the plains of Mesopotamia, Cappadocia, or Bithynia. Question the school-boy as you would at home ; you will find his answers quite familiar to you. You may question him on geography, and you will certainly find, to your surprise, that he knows more of the United States than perhaps of his own native country. Question him about social order, he will tell you all men are created equal. *Indeed, what Dr. Hamlin is silently doing with his Robert College, and the American missionary with his Theological Seminary and school-books, all European diplomatists united cannot overbalance.* Having seen all this, you will certainly not be astonished if you see Yankee clocks; American chairs, tables, organs; American agricultural implements; Yankee cotton-gins, saw-mills, sewing-machines; American flowers in the very heart of Kurdistan; Yankee saddles, and a Yankee rider on the wild mountains of Asia Minor, perhaps singing, with his native companion, some familiar tune. Be not surprised if you be invited to a prayer-meeting on these mountains, where you hear the congregation singing *Old Hundred*, as heartily as you have ever heard it at home. You will certainly own then, if you have not before, that the American people have a sacred interest in this country."

The European Turkey mission, separately organized in 1871, and using Constantinople as its center of publication, deserves a few words, by reason of its prospective importance. The country was explored, and a small beginning made, as long ago as 1858. In that year Mr. Morse entered Adrianople; but his books and two thousand copies of the Turkish Testament were seized by the authorities. When, on remonstrance of the British and American consuls, the Porte ordered the surrender of the books, the desponding utterance of the Turkish officials was well worthy of notice: "If it is the will of God that the Bible prevail, let his will be done."

The mission is directed primarily not to Turks, but to Bulgarians, a people numbering perhaps five or six millions. They belong to the Slavonic race, and nominally to the Greek church. They are a pastoral people, neat, amiable, and industrious, but uneducated and uninquiring. Early attempts to awaken their interest were unsuccessful and discouraging. But with the continuance of these efforts, the intrusion of macadamized roads, railways, and civilization, a change has taken place. Education begins to be prized, and forty young Bulgarians are in Robert college. Everything is now in readiness for a vigorous campaign, if the Christian soldiers can be found. The field is thoroughly explored. The strong points are designated, and three stations occupied. A complete Bulgarian Bible — the fruit of Mr. Riggs's twelve years' toil — is ready ; and there is a wide-spread desire to obtain it. A few converts are scattered here and there, and a young and active church is just organized. Two other hopeful signs are seen : The spirit of persecution has been awakened at Yamboul ; and at Bansko an earnest written demand for light in the Greek church itself — for elevation of the schools, for the observance of the Sabbath, for religious services in the language of the people, and " that the teachings of the gospel be preached."

Here everything seems now ready for the sickle. If the laborers can but be furnished, and the enterprise pushed as the greatness of the opportunity requires, we may well watch, and pray, and hope for cheering results. It is a mission on which to look with an intelligent interest, for itself and for its relations.

March, 1876.

The statistics of the missions given in the foregoing sketch are from reports forwarded in 1871. A new edition being called for it was thought best to use the stereotype plates as they were, appending a few paragraphs in regard to the condition of the missions as reported in 1875. No special change has occurred within the last four years in methods of labor, and there has been less of progress than might have been expected in some of the fields if more laborers and more means could have been furnished from America, or if, on the other hand, the native Protestant communities had been less embarrassed by poverty, the sore oppression, in the way of taxes, incident to the present financial condition and policy of the Turkish government, and the terrible famine of 1874–5, in portions of Asia Minor. The progress, however, has been considerable, and the present prospects of the work are perhaps quite as cheering as could be expected, aside from financial perplexities. Here, as in other mission fields, there has been much advance in the department of woman's work for woman.

Connected with the *European Turkey mission* there are now ten ordained missionaries and twelve female assistant missionaries. Two of the missionaries engaged specially in translating and other literary work, reside at Constantinople ; the others at three stations more fully in the field, — Eski Zagra, Samokov, and Monastir. There are seven out-stations, three churches — two of them at out-stations — with about one hundred members, three native pastors, eight licensed preachers, four teachers, and five other native helpers. A Theological School at Samokov, reports eleven students, and the female boarding school thirty, — twenty-two of them boarders. The missionaries feel that " the period of growth " has come in this field. Changes for the better have been rapid for a few years past, and specially so for the last year reported.

In connection with the *Western Turkey mission* the full establishment of what is called the " Home " at Constantinople, mainly a female seminary, for which a fine building has been erected, through the efforts of the Woman's Board of Missions, is an event of much interest. Other

boarding schools for girls, at Marsovan, Manissa, and
Baghchejuk are doing a good work, and the Theological
Seminary at Marsovan is of great value to the churches
of this field. The mission now occupies six stations, —
Constantinople, Manissa, Broosa, Marsovan, Cesarea, and
Sivas, — with 63 out-stations. There are 24 organized
churches, with 1,086 members, 11 native pastors, 25 licensed preachers, and 75 teachers; 64 pupils in theological schools and station classes, 147 in female boarding
schools, and 2,558 in common schools. The printing by
the mission press amounted in 1874 to 1,784,620 pages,
making a total from the beginning of 300,436,800 pages.

In *Central Turkey* it has been thought best to reduce
the number of places occupied as stations, and since 1872
only two stations have been reported — Aintab and
Marash. But there are 29 out-stations, 26 organized
churches with not far from 2,400 members (the returns
are not complete), 19 ordained native ministers, 19 other
licensed preachers, and 50 teachers. The Theological
Seminary at Marash, and the seminary for girls at Aintab,
are doing a work of great value, and an earnest effort is
in progress to secure a full endowment, and good buildings for a college at Aintab. Over $50,000 have been
secured for this object, in Turkey, England, and the United
States, — more than $7,000 having been contributed by
the people of Aintab.

In *Eastern Turkey*, Van has been occupied as a station
since 1872. This city has been called " the Sevastopol of
the Armenian Church," and the brethren had long wished
to see mission families stationed there. There are supposed to be about 20,000 Armenians in the city — the
whole population being not far from 35,000 — and perhaps 30,000 more within a day's ride; but the opposition
to evangelical religion is not likely to be easily overcome.

The other stations now occupied by this mission are Erzroom, Harpoot, and Mardin, Bitlis having been included in the Van station field. The out-stations of the mission number 114. The churches are 30, with a total membership of 1,567. Nineteen of these churches have native pastors, and there are 30 other native preachers, 95 teachers, and 63 helpers. Forty students are reported in the Theological Seminary at Harpoot and the station training classes at Erzroom and Bitlis; a normal school at Harpoot has 57 pupils; three girls' boarding schools at Erzroom, Harpoot, and Mardin, have 72; "other adults," to the number of 432, are reported as under instruction, while the scholars in 99 common schools number almost 3,600. The missionaries feel that the time has come when education in this field also should be farther advanced by establishing a college.

The whole working force in the four missions in Turkey, by the latest returns, was as follows: ordained missionaries 52; male assistant missionaries 4; females 81; native pastors 52; native preachers 82; native teachers 224; other helpers 102. The churches were 83, with more than 5,000 members, and the whole number of adults and children under instruction is not far from 8,700.

MISSIONARIES, 1876.	Went Out.	Station.
EUROPEAN TURKEY MISSION.		
Rev. Elias Riggs, D. D., LL. D. . . .	1832	Constantinople.
Mrs. Martha J. Riggs	1832	
Rev. James F. Clarke	1859	Samokov.
Mrs. Isabella G. Clarke	1859	
Rev. Lewis Bond, Jr.	1868	Eski Zagra.
Mrs. Fannie G. Bond	1868	
Rev. William E. Locke	1868	Samokov.
Mrs. Zoe A. M. Locke	1868	
Rev. Henry P. Page	1868	Eski Zagra.
Mrs. Mary A. Page	1868	
Miss Esther T. Maltbie	1870	Samokov.
Mrs. Anna V. Mumford	1871	Samokov.
Rev. George D. Marsh	1872	Eski Zagra.
Mrs. Ursula C. Marsh	1875	
Rev. J. W. Baird	1872	Monastir.
Mrs. Ellen Baird	1870	
Rev. J. Henry House	1872	Samokov.
Mrs. Addie S. House	1872	
Rev. Edward W. Jenney	1873	Monastir.
Mrs. Kate M. Jenney	1873	
Rev. Theodore L. Byington	1874	Constantinople.
Mrs. Margaret E. Byington . . .	1874	
MISSION TO WESTERN TURKEY.		
Rev. Benjamin Schneider, D. D. . . .	1833	Marsovan.
Mrs. Susan M. Schneider	1858	
Rev. George W. Wood, D. D. . . .	1838	Constantinople.
Mrs. Sarah A. H. Wood	1871	
Rev. Edwin E. Bliss, D. D.	1843	Constantinople.
Mrs. Isabella H. Bliss	1843	
Rev. Justin W. Parsons	1850	Bardezag.
Mrs. Catherine Parsons	1850	
Rev. Wilson A. Farnsworth	1852	Cesarea.
Mrs. Caroline E. Farnsworth . . .	1852	
Rev. Sanford Richardson	1854	Broosa.
Mrs. Rhoda M. Richardson	1854	
Rev. Ira F. Pettibone	1855	Constantinople.
Rev. Julius Y. Leonard	1857	Marsovan.
Mrs. Amelia A. Leonard	1857	
Rev. Joseph K. Greene	1859	Constantinople.
Mrs. Elizabeth A. Greene	1859	
Rev. George F. Herrick	1859	Constantinople.
Mrs. Helen M. Herrick	1859	
Rev. John F. Smith	1863	Marsovan.
Mrs. Laura E. Smith	1863	
Miss Eliza Fritcher	1863	Marsovan.
Mrs. Elizabeth Giles	1864	Cesarea.
Rev. Theodore A. Baldwin . . .	1867	Manissa.

MISSIONARIES, 1876.	Went Out.	Station.
MISSION TO WESTERN TURKEY, *continued.*		
Mrs. Matilda J. Baldwin	1867	Manissa.
Rev. Charles C. Tracy	1867	Marsovan.
Mrs. L. A. Tracy	1867	
Rev. Lyman Bartlett	1867	Cesarea.
Mrs. Cornelia C. Bartlett	1867	
Miss Sarah A. Closson	1867	Cesarea.
Mr. H. O. Dwight	1867	Constantinople.
Mrs. Ardelle M. Dwight	1869	
Miss Flavia S. Bliss	1868	Sivas.
Rev. Milan H. Hitchcock	1869	Constantinople.
Mrs. Lucy A. Hitchcock	1869	
Rev. Edward Riggs	1869	Sivas.
Mrs. Sarah H. Riggs	1869	
Rev. J. O. Barrows	1869	Manissa.
Mrs. Clara S. Barrows	1869	
Miss Julia A. Rappleye	1870	Broosa.
Miss Cornelia P. Dwight	1871	Constantinople.
Miss Laura Farnham	1871	Bardezag.
Miss Phœbe L. Cull	1871	Manissa.
Miss Mary M. Patrick	1871	Constantinople.
Miss Fannie E. Washburne	1872	Marsovan.
Miss Charlotte L. Noyes	1872	Constantinople.
Rev. A. W. Hubbard	1873	Sivas.
Mrs. Emma R. Hubbard	1873	
Miss Electa C. Parsons	1873	Constantinople.
Mrs. Cora W. Tomson	1873	Constantinople.
Rev. Marcellus Bowen	1874	Constantinople.
Mrs. Flora P. Bowen	1874	
Rev. Charles H. Brooks	1874	Manissa.
Mrs. Fannie W. Brooks	1874	
Mrs. Kate P. Williams	1875	Constantinople.
Rev. Daniel Staver	1875	Cesarea.
Mrs. Abbie S. Staver	1875	
Rev. Charles C. Stearns	1875	Manissa.
Mrs. Sophie D. Stearns	1875	Manissa.
Miss Hattie G. Powers	1875	Manissa.
Miss Ellen C. Parsons	1875	Constantinople.
MISSION TO CENTRAL TURKEY.		
David H. Nutting, M. D.	1854	Kessab.
Mrs. Mary E. Nutting	1854	
Rev. T. C. Trowbridge	1855	Aintab.
Mrs. Margaret R. Trowbridge		
Mrs. J. L. Coffing	1857	Marash.
Miss Myra A. Proctor	1859	Aintab.
Rev. Giles F. Montgomery	1863	Marash.
Mrs. Emily R. Montgomery	1863	
Rev. L. H. Adams	1865	Kessab.
Mrs. Nancy D. Adams	1866	
Rev. Henry T. Perry	1866	Marash.

34   SKETCHES OF THE MISSIONS.

MISSIONARIES, 1876.	Went Out.	Station.
MISSION TO CENTRAL TURKEY, *continued.*		
Mrs. Jennie H. Perry	1866	Marash.
Miss Mary G. Hollister	1867	Aintab.
Rev. Henry Marden	1869	Aintab.
Miss Mary S. Williams	1871	Marash.
Miss Corinna Shattuck	1873	Aintab.
Rev. Americus Fuller	1874	Aintab.
Mrs. Amelia D. Fuller	1874	
Rev. Edward G. Bickford	1874	Marash.
Mrs. Harriet S. Bickford	1874	
Miss Ellen M. Pierce	1874	Aintab.
Miss Charlotte D. Spencer	1875	Marash.
MISSION TO EASTERN TURKEY.		
Rev. George C. Knapp	1855	Bitlis.
Mrs. Alzina M. Knapp	1855	
Rev. O. P. Allen	1855	Harpoot.
Mrs. Caroline R. Allen	1855	
Rev. Crosby H. Wheeler	1857	Harpoot.
Mrs. Susan A. Wheeler	1857	
Rev. Herman N. Barnum, D. D. . . .	1858	Harpoot.
Mrs. Mary E. Barnum		
Rev. Moses P. Parmelee	1863	Erzroom.
Mrs. Julia F. Parmelee	1871	
Miss Hattie Seymour	1867	Harpoot.
Rev. Henry S. Barnum	1867	Van.
Mrs. Helen P. Barnum	1869	
Rev. A. N. Andrus	1868	Mardin.
Mrs. Olive L. Andrus	1868	
Miss Charlotte E. Ely	1868	Bitlis.
Miss M. A. C. Ely	1868	Bitlis.
Miss Cyrene O. Van Duzee . . .	1868	Erzroom.
Rev. J. E. Pierce	1868	Erzroom.
Mrs. Lizzie A. Pierce	1868	
Rev. R. M. Cole	1868	Erzroom.
Mrs. Lizzie Cole	1868	
George C. Raynolds, M. D.	1869	Van.
Mrs. Martha W. Raynolds	1869	
Miss Caroline E. Bush	1870	Harpoot.
Rev. J. E. Scott	1872	Van.
Mrs. Annie E. Scott	1872	
Rev. Newton H. Bell	1874	Mardin.
Mrs. Emily H. Bell	1874	
Daniel M. B. Thom, M. D.	1874	Mardin.
Mrs. L. H. Thom	1874	
Miss Sarah E. Sears	1874	Mardin.
Rev. John K. Browne	1875	Harpoot.
Miss Clarissa H. Pratt	1875	Mardin.

Religion in America
Series II

An Arno Press Collection

Adler, Felix. **Creed and Deed:** A Series of Discourses. New York, 1877.

Alexander, Archibald. **Evidences of the Authenticity, Inspiration, and Canonical Authority of the Holy Scriptures.** Philadelphia, 1836.

Allen, Joseph Henry. **Our Liberal Movement in Theology:** Chiefly as Shown in Recollections of the History of Unitarianism in New England. 3rd edition. Boston, 1892.

American Temperance Society. **Permanent Temperance Documents of the American Temperance Society.** Boston, 1835.

American Tract Society. **The American Tract Society Documents,** 1824-1925. New York, 1972.

Bacon, Leonard. **The Genesis of the New England Churches.** New York, 1874.

Bartlett, S[amuel] C. **Historical Sketches of the Missions of the American Board.** New York, 1972.

Beecher, Lyman. **Lyman Beecher and the Reform of Society:** Four Sermons, 1804-1828. New York, 1972.

[Bishop, Isabella Lucy Bird.] **The Aspects of Religion in the United States of America.** London, 1859.

Bowden, James. **The History of the Society of Friends in America.** London, 1850, 1854. Two volumes in one.

Briggs, Charles Augustus. **Inaugural Address and Defense,** 1891-1893. New York, 1972.

Colwell, Stephen. **The Position of Christianity in the United States,** in Its Relations with Our Political Institutions, and Specially with Reference to Religious Instruction in the Public Schools. Philadelphia, 1854.

Dalcho, Frederick. **An Historical Account of the Protestant Episcopal Church, in South-Carolina,** from the First Settlement of the Province, to the War of the Revolution. Charleston, 1820.

Elliott, Walter. **The Life of Father Hecker.** New York, 1891.

Gibbons, James Cardinal. **A Retrospect of Fifty Years.** Baltimore, 1916. Two volumes in one.

Hammond, L[ily] H[ardy]. **Race and the South:** Two Studies, 1914-1922. New York, 1972.

Hayden, A[mos] S. **Early History of the Disciples in the Western Reserve, Ohio;** With Biographical Sketches of the Principal Agents in their Religious Movement. Cincinnati, 1875.

Hinke, William J., editor. **Life and Letters of the Rev. John Philip Boehm:** Founder of the Reformed Church in Pennsylvania, 1683-1749. Philadelphia, 1916.

Hopkins, Samuel. **A Treatise on the Millennium.** Boston, 1793.

Kallen, Horace M. **Judaism at Bay:** Essays Toward the Adjustment of Judaism to Modernity. New York, 1932.

Kreider, Harry Julius. **Lutheranism in Colonial New York.** New York, 1942.

Loughborough, J. N. **The Great Second Advent Movement:** Its Rise and Progress. Washington, 1905.

M'Clure, David and Elijah Parish. **Memoirs of the Rev. Eleazar Wheelock, D.D.** Newburyport, 1811.

McKinney, Richard I. **Religion in Higher Education Among Negroes.** New Haven, 1945.

Mayhew, Jonathan. **Observations on the Charter and Conduct of the Society for the Propagation of the Gospel in Foreign Parts;** Designed to Shew Their Non-conformity to Each Other. Boston, 1763.

Mott, John R. **The Evangelization of the World in this Generation.** New York, 1900.

Payne, Bishop Daniel A. **Sermons and Addresses,** 1853-1891. New York, 1972.

Phillips, C[harles] H. **The History of the Colored Methodist Episcopal Church in America:** Comprising Its Organization, Subsequent Development, and Present Status. Jackson, Tenn., 1898.

Reverend Elhanan Winchester: Biography and Letters. New York, 1972.

Riggs, Stephen R. **Tah-Koo Wah-Kan; Or, the Gospel Among the Dakotas.** Boston, 1869.

Rogers, Elder John. **The Biography of Eld. Barton Warren Stone, Written by Himself:** With Additions and Reflections. Cincinnati, 1847.

Booth-Tucker, Frederick. **The Salvation Army in America:** Selected Reports, 1899-1903. New York, 1972.

Satolli, Francis Archbishop. **Loyalty to Church and State.** Baltimore, 1895.

Schaff, Philip. **Church and State in the United States** or the American Idea of Religious Liberty and its Practical Effects with Official Documents. New York and London, 1888. (Reprinted from *Papers of the American Historical Association,* Vol. II, No. 4.)

Smith, Horace Wemyss. **Life and Correspondence of the Rev. William Smith, D.D.** Philadelphia, 1879, 1880. Two volumes in one.

Spalding, M[artin] J. **Sketches of the Early Catholic Missions of Kentucky;** From Their Commencement in 1787 to the Jubilee of 1826-7. Louisville, 1844.

Steiner, Bernard C., editor. **Rev. Thomas Bray:** His Life and Selected Works Relating to Maryland. Baltimore, 1901. (Reprinted from *Maryland Historical Society Fund Publication,* No. 37.)

To Win the West: Missionary Viewpoints, 1814-1815. New York, 1972.

Wayland, Francis and H. L. Wayland. **A Memoir of the Life and Labors of Francis Wayland, D.D., LL.D.** New York, 1867. Two volumes in one.

Willard, Frances E. **Woman and Temperance:** Or, the Work and Workers of the Woman's Christian Temperance Union. Hartford, 1883.

DUE

MAR 0 7

NO

30 505 JOS

50508